A CLASSIC CHINESE READER

MASTERS ON MASTERPIECES OF CHINESE CALLIGRAPHY

COMPILED
BY EDITORIAL BOARD
OF CHINESE LITERATURE AND HISTORY

TRANSLATED BY YANG SHUQING AND LI HUIJIAO

CHINA INTERCONTINENTAL PRESS   ZHONGHUA BOOK COMPANY

The Origin, Necessity and
Importance of Calligraphy

Before talking about calligraphy skills, I need to explain an extremely important fact.

Calligraphy is not created by a single ancient sage who asks his followers to obey his will but exists instinctively in each stroke of Chinese characters. With the cooperation of flexible human wrists and appropriate tools, it happens naturally and shows up vividly through characters. Creatively, calligraphy cannot be created until after years

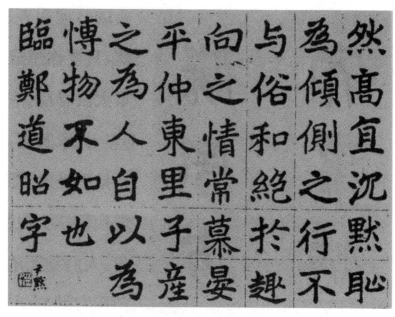

Shen Yinmo's Copy of *Zheng Wengong Stele*

of great efforts in learning and teaching. The rules, universally accepted by calligraphers, are man-made. Here are several examples that can make it easier to understand that the rules are necessary. Only by following the rules can achievements and development be realized.

Grammar, like language, is not created by people before they learn to speak. On the contrary, grammar evolves gradually with the development of language from simple to complex. It exists in the language itself. But with grammar, we can use language skills for constant progress because we can organize increasingly rich vocabulary to express right ideas.

Shen Yinmo's seal script work

Let's have a look at the rhyme of classical poetry. Poets since the Qi and Liang dynasties have chosen sentences with the most harmonious level and oblique tones (lüju in Chinese) and have made up new styles of poetry that is not as serious in rhyme as Regulated Verse. Taking one of the Nineteen Old Poems as an example, *qīng qīng hé pàn cǎo* (three level and two oblique), *shí qǔ tīng qí zhēn* (three oblique and two level), *jí yàn yú xīn yì* (two oblique, two level, and one oblique), *xīn shēng mìao rù shén* (two level, two oblique, and one level).

The Regulated Verse is composed of four sentences with level tone and oblique tone matching. That's how the pattern of the Regulated Verse is shaped from the Four Masters of early Tang Dynasty (Wang Bo, Yang Jiong, Lu Zhaolin, Luo Binwang), Song Zhiwen, Shen Quanqi, Du Shenyan to Du Fu. The rhyme of the Regulated Verse has existed since the emergence of Five-Character poetry. Later generations find it, regard it as a rule, and develop it as classical poetry.

Writing is a small skill, but it has its own rule. We should know that the rule of the writing styles is inherent and it does not depend on our will, so will not change with our likes or dislikes. As long as you want to be a calligrapher and write good Chinese characters, you must take it as a fundamental law and never violate it.

As we all know, there is an objective rule for everything in the universe, be it big or small, natural, social or logical.

It has already been proven by modern practice. Now that the rule is objective, we cannot change it at will but we can fully understand it, master it, and make use of it to get everything done. It is certain that those who cannot take advantage of writing rules cannot write well. But it is also true that those who can write do not necessarily know writing rules. We need to make it clear when the topic is discussed later.

Stele and Rubbing

Qi Gong

At first, I need to explain the two words in the title. What is stele? It is actually a short stone. What is it for? Erecting such a stone in front of a tomb was originally to fix ropes so that a coffin could be put into the pit. Let's leave the function alone. Words were written on the stone to show who was buried. This is another function. Later, it was used for some other purposes. People might erect a stele for a living person, such as a local ruler, to record his exploits and honors. The words on such a commemorative

A stele form of Tang Dynasty

stele are called inscriptions. Why did people make them? To inform people why the stele was made and who it was made for. Therefore, the words on the stele should be ones that everyone can read and should be written in ways that everyone can recognize.

At the outset, those who made the inscriptions on the stele were not necessarily celebrities, calligraphers, scholars or officials. All they needed to do was write clearly. It can be terrible if nobody can identify their writings. That is why Chinese characters on the stele are all in a standard script. In the early Tang Dynasty (618-907), Emperor Taizong of Tang (Li Shimin, ruling from 626 to 649) was so fond of calligraphy that he learned from Wang Xizhi. He wrote in *xingshu* (semi-cursive script). Maybe he did not know how to write in *kaishu* (regular script) or was not good at it. He inscribed two steles, both in *xingshu*: one was *Hot Spring Inscription* and the other *Jin Ancestral Temple Inscription*. His son Li Zhi also inscribed steles for many ministers in such writing style. It was from then on that *xingshu* began to appear on steles.

7

Empress Wu Zetian (ruling from 690 to 705) erected a stele for her gigolo (sort of lover) Zhang Changzong and said that he was the reincarnation of Wang Zijin. She had the tomb of Wang Zijin dug up in Dongshan but could not prove whether it was Wang Zijin or not. So she let people erect a stele there, known as *Stele for the Ascended Immortal Prince*. The Chinese characters on the stele were all written in *caoshu* (cursive script), marking that *caoshu* began to appear on steles. Since then, people started to use *caoshu* to transcribe books, essays and Buddhist scriptures. For example, the *Treatise of Calligraphy* by Sun Guoting was written in *caoshu*, so were the phenomena and individual theories of Yogacara (literally "yoga practice"). Such a trend surely influenced the writing styles in this era. However, *kaishu* was still dominant in stele inscription.

Hot Spring Inscription by Emperor Taizong of Tang (partial)

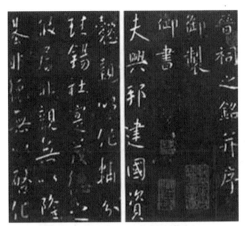

Jin Ancestral Temple Inscription by Emperor Taizong of Tang (partial)

Why? *Xingshu* or *caoshu* could not be identified by a majority of readers.

Later Zhao Mengfu wrote in *kaishu* but exhibited some *xingshu* features. The Chinese characters he wrote were either serious at every stroke or squared ones like those on the Buddhist Steles of the Six Dynasties (222–589). Especially in the late Qing Dynasty, inscribing steles was very popular and on the steles were all squared Chinese characters. Those who inscribed steles were called *beixue* (literally stele scholars). The name started with Ruan Yuan during the reign of Emperor Daoguang of the Qing Dynasty (1644-1911). Later Ye Changchi, Yang Shoujing and Kang Youwei all regarded stele inscriptions as noble and perfect. Actually the styles of stele inscriptions have been changing along the history. With the original *kaishu*, later *xingshu* and *caoshu*, the stele inscriptions cannot fully represent the writing styles of the Six Dynasties.

Are all the Chinese characters on the steles standard? If so, what about "Stele for the Ascended Immortal Prince" by Empress Wu Zetian? What about the *Hot Spring*

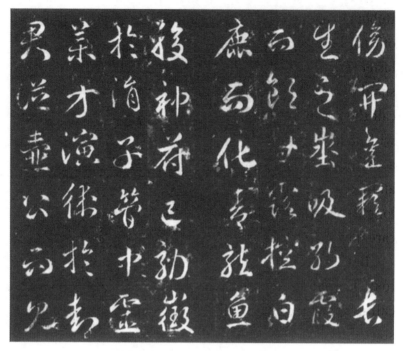

Stele for the Ascended Immortal Prince by Wu Zetian (partial)

Inscription and the *Jin Ancestral Temple Inscription*? So the meaning that the *beixue* conveys is neither complete nor logical.

Now let's talk about rubbing. What is rubbing? It is originally a "note", *"Bian Tiao"* in Beijing dialect, which is just a note written casually. I can write a simple note to someone to tell him/her when I am free and we can meet. This is called a "note". It was originally used among friends, not seriously. During the Six dynasties, a number of Wang Xizhi's notes were passed down. Most of them had only two or three lines. Some only had one line.

Rubbing can also be a letter. If you write a letter to a high official, he should write something back at the end of the letter. For instance, if the official was invited to visit, he should write *"ji ke lai"* (I am coming) to make a reply. We call the letter "writing note". It actually has nothing to do with stele. Stele provides information in a formal way while a writing note is not that serious. We write to each other and we understand the meanings. That is all we need. As long as we can identify the Chinese characters, we do not care how messy they are.

But a writing note, just a piece of paper, can be easily lost. Emperor Taizong of Tang loved Wang Xizhi's calligraphies and collected them. Indeed, the collection started as early as Emperor Wu of Liang (ruling from 502 to 549). He made a scroll out of the scattered notes. There was a letter written by Wang Xizhi to a local official Zhou Fu. It was more than one *zhang* (a traditional Chinese unit of length equal to 3–3.7 m) long. The letter began with *"shi qi ri"* (17th day), a date to show time. Later people called it *Shi qi tie* (literally 17 letters). It was not correct, because the "shi qi" here did not mean there were seventeen notes but it was written in the seventeenth day of the month. So the name did not make sense. It actually consisted of notes with two or three lines and such letters began to gain popularity since then. Till the Song Dynasty (960-1279), *Chunhua Pavilion Model Calligraphy* appeared. It consisted of Chinese characters from the Six Dynasties,

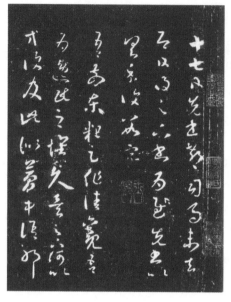

A Letter Beginning with Seventeen by Wang Xizhi (partial)

Han Dynasty and those of Cang Jie. Some were fake and added just to make up the numbers. It was originally inscribed in the pavilion (Emperor's secret library) during the Chunhua period (990-994) of the Northern Song Dynasty. There were many writings of ancient people inscribed here, of which some were authentic and some were fake. The scratchy *Chunhua Pavilion Model Calligraphy* was carved over and over again. But none of them were well-made, vivid or beautiful but rather common and plain. Therefore, rubbing is not necessarily vulgar and stele is not necessarily exquisite; and Wang Xizhi's Chinese characters are not necessarily squared. Remember the debate some time ago? Some people said that the *Lanting Xu* (*Preface to the Poems Collected from the Orchid Pavilion*) was fake just because the Chinese characters were not squared. Let's leave the topic alone.

That is the stele and rubbing. Inscribing steles is not necessarily noble or orthodox. It is very ridiculous for some people to write a note or letter in the way of inscribing steles. In that case, they have to write stroke after stroke and it must be very time-consuming. There was such a person in the Qing Dynasty called Jiang Sheng who wrote letters to others in *zhuanshu* (seal script). He asked his servant to buy some stuff and wrote him a note in *lishu* (clerical script); he asked the cook to buy vegetables and wrote him a list which the cook said he could not read. Jiang Sheng answered that "I wrote in *lishu*, a character style for you *nuli* (slave, *li* in *lishu* and *nuli* is the same character but with different meanings in Chinese); if you cannot read it, you do not deserve to be my slave or cook." This is a joke of Jiang Sheng. Do I have to make a note as simple as *"Qing ni lai yi tang"* (please come) look like Buddhist steles of the Six Dynasties? No. Notes are actually used between friends and acquaintances. If the receiver can understand my writings, it does not matter how messy they are or even they look like passwords. Of course, there is a common standard or habit even for the notes in *caoshu*.

Therefore, stele and rubbing differ in functions rather than positions. Similarly, I use spoon to drink soup and chopsticks to eat dishes. But you cannot say that spoon is higher-grade or better than chopsticks, because you need both when eating. Such examples abound, such as clothes and daily necessities. I will hold an umbrella when it rains and will not do that when it doesn't rain. It doesn't make

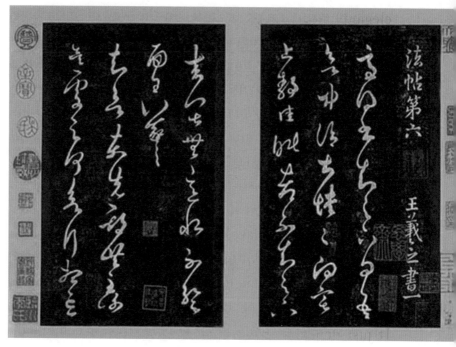

Chunhua Pavilion Model Calligraphy

sense to say those holding umbrellas are superior and the others are vulgar. They just differ in tools, symbols or uses. For example, the notation to record music has developed from numbered musical notation, 1234, musical notation to phonograph disc, audio tape and CDs. Which one is the most ancient? The earliest is Gongche notation on which musical notation is written beside each Chinese character..., and you sing the characters according to the notation. Then among Gongche notation, numbered musical notation, musical notation, phonograph disc, audio tape and CD, which one is ancient and which one is elegant? Gongche notation is the most ancient. Is it the most elegant? Now you already have CDs but you must write down Gongche notation to sing old melodies. Are you elegant? I do not think elegance and vulgarity can be evaluated in this way.

Art styles are consistent with hobbies. I am not against the existing art style. For example, we now live in a *siheyuan* (courtyard house) with tiles on top and windows, doors, and pillars below. It is different from the western-style building but it will be fine whether to live in the western-style building or *siheyuan*, or other buildings. Similarly, I do not think there is any difference if I wear Chinese-style shirt and pants or I wear a suit. It just depends on occasions and we cannot say which one is better or more elegant. Some people like Buddhist steles such as those in the Wu Liang Shrine, the carving of which is very clumsy and original. Some people are particular fond of wood engraving. It is actually no big deal. Some people like opera costumes and facial masks, but I think that ordinary people's faces look better. A natural makeup can make a person more beautiful but a fancy and messy face with red and green lines can be confusing. Can you image drawing the Taiji diagram and many patterns on the Justice Bao's (Bao Zheng, whose face is known to be black) face? Someone likes it very much and I am not against it. He/She can keep it even though I will not go out with a painted face. If I make up and look like a *dougen*

On Calligraphy, Entry 97, by Qi Gong

(the main speaker of Comic Dialogue) and you get your face painted black like Justice Bao, we will not be allowed to attend the meeting today. They may wonder what we are doing. The question is that I am not against you to fall for it. You have your freedom but I will not follow you. Practices and personal hobbies (or preferences) are two different things. If I write Chinese characters in a fancy style on signboards, I will have more freedom because I write in ways I like. But I will first draw some lines with a ruler and pencil to show the outline of each stroke so that I can make the fancy effect more obvious. Anyway I will not write in this way when I write a note or letter, for it takes too long. I am not against personal hobbies of art styles or preferences for some ancient and immature writing styles (or writing styles existing during the process of becoming mature). However, we cannot impose what we like on someone else, nor can we tell them that they have to do it in this way to be superior.

How to Choose Steles and Rubbings to Learn

Qi Gong

Now I am going to talk about how to choose steles and rubbings to learn. I am often asked which stele or rubbing is suitable for learning. This is not an easy question. I often say that you can learn whatever you have or whatever you like. Similarly, if I want a girlfriend, I ask someone for advice: Should I date a plump or slim one? What about her age, province or major? However experienced the person might be, he cannot help with such problems. It is the same for calligraphy learning. Which kind of calligraphy should I learn first? I have met a lot of people who will say, "Ah, you should learn *zhuanshu* (seal script) first; when you have learned it well enough, you begin with *lishu* (clerical script) and then *kaishu* (regular script)". I have taken great efforts in answering the question over and over again and I truly hate the opinion

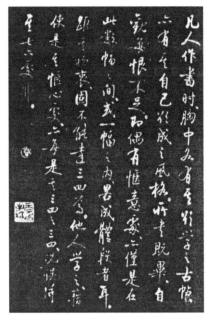

One of *On Calligraphy Notes* by Qi Gong

above. I just wonder when I should have learnt *zhuanshu* or *lishu* well enough. Is there a teacher to score my *zhuanshu* and let me pass to begin with *lishu* learning? Who is it? Some people have written in one style all through their life but their writings are not good enough. Then they will never get the chance to learn a second writing style during the rest of their life. How can we solve the problem? I do not think there is a definite standard. For example, if you want to learn to write, you should learn to make knots first. Not until you have totally mastered the knot methods can you begin with writing. I do not think it makes sense.

There are another group of people who take drawing

19

boards to paint in the park (or somewhere else) where tree peonies and herbaceous peonies are blooming. If they ask the passers-by: should I paint tree peony or herbaceous peony? The answer they get must be: you can paint whatever you want, because it's not my business. Similarly, if the people who go to restaurants ask waiters what they should eat. The waiters will be sure to give no definite answers: "You can eat chicken, fish, beef, pork, or mutton. You can order anything after you have made a choice. I can only tell you what we have but I can't help you make a choice." Think about yourself after reading the examples above. Have you ever asked others in the same way: Sir, which kind of rubbings should I learn? Now we have a very convenient method. Go to the bookstore. On the shelves lie a wide variety of rubbings and teaching booklets. You can have a look at and choose from the various rubbings, among which both the Ou (Ouyang Xun) style and Liu (Liu Gongquan) style have more than one version.

What a pity it is that humans are so unconfident in themselves. Especially in writing, most of people I have met lack confidence. Why unconfident? They think it is mysterious. Why mysterious? Someone has told them so: you should not write randomly and you must ask for advice. They are restricted by the exaggeratedly mysterious impression of calligraphy and lose the courage to even have a try, let alone being confident. If I am asked

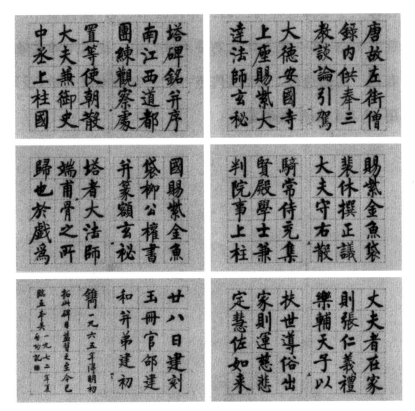

Qi Gong's Copy of *Xuanmi Tower Stele*

the question, I will ask him/her in turn: "which do you like?" If he/she says "I think this one is fine", I will say this one is the right choice. Why bother to ask others? It is just like ordering or dating. You eat what you like and you date who you like. It is normal and easy. Why aren't you confident in terms of writing? Probably some people, especially celebrities, talk about methods of calligraphy and you totally trust them. Honestly speaking, these people have credit (mentoring, of course) but their misleading cannot be ignored.

I have also met such people, young or old, showing great respect to me (as if they were going to kneel before me) and saying "please accept my sincere request and teach me how to write". How? I am not an immortal who can use his magic finger to touch a man's head and make him enlightened at once. They must believe that there exist people who are capable of Midas touch. I have to say that they are too pathetic because they are deluded by such an absurdity and made to believe that calligraphy is too mysterious to reach. You have to get rid of the idea. Just go to the bookstore and read the rubbings on the desks or shelves. You can ask the salesperson for help if the rubbings are out of reach and can also return them if they don't fit you: "Please give me another one". It's no big deal. The rubbings now are so much more resemblant to the original ones compared with those re-inscribed again and again in ancient times. They are printed on the photographic plates and even the black color and dry/wet writings can be identified, looking nearly the same as the original ones. Therefore, you may be interested in imitating them. If you find them no more satisfying after a while, just buy a new one. After all, they are quite affordable. Instead of spending much money on a lot of rice paper to practice, you might as well take the money to buy several rubbings to imitate and write at anytime, better and more effective than those theory books. Which rubbing is the best? I think that you should choose the one you like most, and your interest is allowed to change as well. I was fond of this one yesterday but I find it not appropriate after a while of practice. Then I choose another one. It is all right. But some people may doubt it is inconstant. You must insist on writing even though you are unwilling to do it. Am I inconstant just because I change a rubbing? I will be angry if someone says this to me: What if I am inconstant? There is no prohibition principle and it is no big deal. It is just changing a rubbing or a book. Why can't we have a try? You can choose a rubbing and change it on your own will.

A new problem may emerge after you have already chosen a satisfactory rubbing: I have tried many times but the Chinese characters I write do not look the same as the original ones. Why? I can tell you that you can never write exactly the same as the rubbings. I used to learn to write in my father's writing style but I failed. I used to learn to write in my brother's writing style but I failed again. Then I tried to write in my teacher's writing style and the result was the same. Others may think that the Chinese characters I write may look a little bit like those of my teacher or my father. But you will find the difference after careful analysis. Why? We know that signing papers is effective in law. If Zhang San signs his name on a contract, document or something else, the signature will be legally binding. Any imitations of such signature must be identified by legal experts. Therefore, you mustn't imitate others' signatures.

Why? A cannot write exactly the same as or like those of B. That is why we can tell whether the ancient painting and calligraphy are authentic, fake or copy. Why? It follows special rules. Then why should I learn if I cannot write the same as original ones? This is another question. What you learn is the method. You write in his way and the Chinese characters will look nice; you write against his way and the Chinese characters will look awkward. It is the feature of a celebrity or school. Another school has its own features. We should understand that different schools or celebrities have different writing styles and follow different rules. We learn their methods to produce nice Chinese characters. This is all we need and our characters are not necessarily the same as theirs.

People had no access to good rubbings before. Zhao Mengfu wrote that ancient people could only get rubbings with several lines. That is because there were no photocopies. By carefully studying and imitating each Chinese character on these limited rubbings, they could be acknowledged and praised by the public. It provides important information. We can see how difficult it can be for ancient people to get good rubbings. Let's leave the fact alone that getting several lines of Chinese characters and concentrating on learning can make one famous in ancient times. Don't be disturbed by when you can be famous. What we can easily get today are not several lines of ancient Chinese characters but those written by ancient people themselves, whether in the photo or photocopy, exactly the same as the original ones. Then whether we can write well depends on whether we are focused or not. There is my last point about choosing rubbings to learn. People may put the rubbings in front or on the left to imitate. They look at them and write whatever they see, such as the Chinese characters "tian", "ren", and "di". After finishing, they find them nothing like the original ones and become upset or even annoyed: Why can't I write like the original ones? I think that you need a research at first. Take a piece of transparent paper, or plastic film (dip your brush in ink; the ink does not stick to the film but adding a little bit of soap will work), put the rubbing at the bottom of the film, and outline the Chinese characters through the film. What is it for? It can help you to find how long the distance is between the two horizontal strokes of the Chinese character "tian"; where the left-falling stroke starts, where it turns, and where the right-falling stroke goes. You will understand in this way how the Chinese character "tian" is written. Why we should outline it, you may ask. I want to ask you in return, why you imitate the rubbing. You may write in whatever way you want if you haven't chosen to imitate the rubbings. "I can decide not to imitate them. I just like to write in my way and write randomly. The two horizontal strokes of my Chinese character 'tian' have one *chi* (unit of length, three *chi* equals one meter) in between and the left- and right-falling stroke have one *cun* (unit of length, one-tenth of a *chi*) in between. I just write it in this way and it is none of your business." Yes, you write as you like and I won't argue with you. Now that you admit that you want to learn the rubbings, you have to imitate them first. It is not reliable to measure with your eyes. You write on the paper based on the impression and will find it different from the rubbings. I once said that you'd better put the rubbing on the left, imitate it firstly and outline it with the film secondly. Study the strokes carefully and make sure the precise location of each stroke. What is the relationship between these two strokes and those four strokes? How long is the distance and how long does it last? After the second research, you can write based on your eyes the third time you write. The method adopted for the first time and the third time is the same, but a real research happens between the two attempts. In this way, you write each character three times. Suppose there are a hundred characters, write each one three times in this way. It will be totally different if you try again.

So I think that if you want to learn rubbings you should find the answers to the following questions. Firstly, why can't I write the same as original ones? Secondly, why should I imitate them? I think that one can be creative when choosing and imitating rubbings. You can also follow the ancient ways, absorb the most effective elements, and make full use of them for our creations.

Buddhists use scriptures to cultivate themselves and disseminate the dharma (basic principles of the cosmos). The essence of Buddhism is expressed by the scriptures. Nowadays, there are printed scriptures for monks to recite, disseminate the Buddhist ideas, and proofread. *The Tripitaka* is especially popular among the Buddhists. There are various versions of scriptures in different languages.

When Buddhism was first introduced into China,

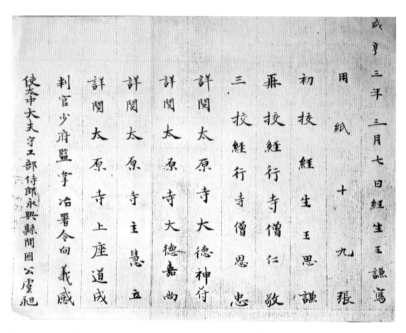

Preface of the third volume of The *Saddharmapundarika-sutra* which is the official transcribed scripture in the early Tang Dynasty (672)

translating and transcribing the scriptures were important because Buddhists used the scriptures to disseminate dharma. At that time, printing had not been invented so the scriptures had to transcribe the scriptures by hands after the scriptures were translated from Sanskrit into Chinese. In order to make them widely spread, lots of people transcribed them by hands. Then, the Buddhists would revise them seriously to make sure there were no misunderstandings and the essence of Buddhism was not distorted.

It was Buddhists' job to transcribe and comment

scriptures. It is said that writing one sentence in the scriptures is equal to doing several deeds. During the turbulent time between the Northern and Southern Dynasties (386-589), Buddhism was widely spread because many people prayed for the blessing of Buddha. There were lots of followers of Buddhism who intended to accumulate merits by spending all of their money in transcribing scriptures. They transcribed the scriptures as donors. Lots of their personal interests were involved . We can find their individual aspirations towards Bodhisattva in the preface of the scriptures. They wished that there would be no more diseases and disasters. People who were far away from home expected to return earlier. People prayed health for their families. They did these for the living as well as the dead. The dedicated officials transcribed the scriptures for the prosperity of the country and the people. Once there was an old man who was more than 83 years old and he made mixture of his blood from his fingers and the ink to transcribe the *Diamond Sutra* (also *Vajracchedika-sutra*). He did it because he wanted to begin his new life as soon as possible. Some people even transcribed scriptures for their cattle and sheep, hoping the animals would get blessed so they would not be domestic animals any more in their future life.

People who transcribed scriptures with individual aspirations had intention to benefit from what they did for the unfortunate people. When they could do nothing with their troubles, they wished to do something related to Buddhism that would help them out of dilemma. The principle, retribution for sin, which was advocated by Buddhists, was used to lead people to be good. The followers of Buddhism had imaginations like the folks. So the principle, retribution for sin, was once regarded as the formula among the common people. Just like the idea that the sun rises from the east. People had no scientific evidence for it but took it as common sense. Sometimes there were incidents which prove the fact that people's dreams would come true because they transcribed the scriptures. Followers of Buddhism would be happy about this. If someone did not get his reward after transcribing the scripture, they would doubt their faithfulness and piety or maybe they would think that they did not transcribe enough. Therefore, some people kept transcribing the scriptures for a long time. As for those who transcribed scriptures for the dead, there was no evidence to show whether they did the right thing or something rewarding. However, those people believed that the day when they accomplished transcribing was the very day for full happiness and fortune. Although there was no substantial evidence to show that their aspirations would became reality, they felt satisfied.

Accumulating merits with purpose of getting reward by transcribing the scriptures was much more economical than building Buddhist grottoes or temples and stupa (a domed edifice housing Buddhist or Jain relics). Transcribing scriptures costs less money. Followers of Buddhism who were not very rich could do that not only because it was costless but also they could do it at any time. The donors would be deemed to be pious enough if they volunteered to transcribe scriptures. While if the donors were illiterate or they were busy with their jobs or they were the superiority with high social status, they would employ someone to transcribe scriptures for them. Scriptures like these were also welcomed by Buddhists in the temples.

We can see from the preface of *Dunhuang Transcribed Scriptures* that there were lots of people engaged in the transcription of scriptures. They were from different social status, including Buddhist monks, followers of Buddhism, scripture transcribers, official scripture transcribers, common people, students in the counties, members of transcribers' teams, people who were familiar with regular script, officials of regular script, and lower class officials. Some of them were followers of Buddhism while others might not be.

At first, donors employed monks to transcribe scriptures. With the popularity of accumulating merits by transcribing scriptures, the number of monks who were able to transcribe could not meet the demand. So those people who took transcription as their jobs were then employed to transcribe scriptures. Gradually, there were a group of people who were professional scripture transcribers. They were just those people who were called transcribers of scripture in *Dunhuang Transcribed Scriptures*. Since then these people began to be called scripture transcribers.

In my opinion, signature of transcriber of scripture firstly appeared in the fourteenth volume of *Satyasiddhi Shastra* that was finished in the fourth year of the Yongping (511) period of the Northern Wei Dynasty (386-557), which belonged to the *Dunhuang Transcribed Scriptures*. Wang Sengqian, a calligrapher of the Southern Qi Dynasty (479-502) wrote in his book that Xie Jing and Xie Fu were capable to transcribe scripture and they were able to understand the essence of the scripture. These two people whose family names were Xie were lower-class officials and they took transcribing scripture as their jobs. Wang Sengqian died in the third year of Yongming (485) of the Southern Qi Dynasty. So it can be concluded that transcribing scripture firstly became a profession in the fifth century. Juqu Anzhou, an emperor of the Northern Liang Dynasty (401-439), once employed someone to transcribe scriptures for him in the seventh year of the Chengping (449). The transcriber signed in the scripture like this: Transcribed by Zhang Xiuzu. Zhang Xiuzu was a scripture transcriber who led a destitute life in the southern of the Northern Liang Dynasty.

Scripture transcriber took transcribing as their

profession. Tai Jingnong, a literary critic and a calligrapher of modern time once stated in his book *On Scripture Transcriber* that scripture transcriber should be responsible since they started to transcribe the Buddhist scripture and they were paid by the employers. So they should be pious to the Bodhisattva and they were supposed to be careful with their transcription. Donors paid money for scripture transcribers with the purpose that their aspirations could become reality. However, whether their aspirations could become reality was dependent on several factors, such as the mental state of the transcribers and their calligraphy and behaviors and surroundings. There was a saying that if the scripture transcribers were not so pious they could not cultivate themselves in a Buddhist way and they might make mistakes in their transcriptions. Surroundings of transcribers were also important. Some people lived in shabby houses and were disturbed by insects, but they were not afraid. However, their transcribed scriptures could not be used to relieve people who were suffering, because these scriptures were believed to be less effective. If so, the donors would lose their money and the chance to accumulate merits. The scriptures written by scripture transcribers would be used by the Buddhists. If the scripture transcribers did their jobs carelessly and only wanted to get the payment, the Buddhists would not take their works. So someone made forbidding statements of scripture transcription. The first one stressed that scripture

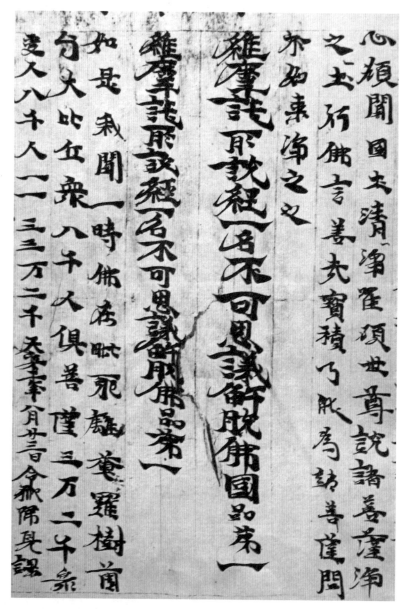

The *Vimalakīrtinirdeśa-sūtra* of the Northern Wei Dynasty
(467, collected in the Dun Huang Research Institute)

transcribers should be responsible for their works and they should be serious when they did transcription, meanwhile it was their responsibility to make sure about the fluency of the scriptures and clarity of the structure. The second one was about warning, saying that if they dealt with the scriptures carelessly they would be punished. While these two statements were just about the spiritual aspects of scripture transcribers, the effective one is the third one, which is to proofread the scriptures. Usually, There were monks would proofread the scriptures according to the original ones. If there were no mistakes, they would make signature to prove that there were no mistakes in the transcribed scriptures. This happened when individuals employed others to transcribe for them.

Official proofreading of newly introduced transcribed Buddhist scriptures in the early Tang Dynasty (618—907) was so strict. Many supervisors were engaged in such proofreading to correct the characters and the meanings. Each of these supervisors must sign their names in the transcribed scriptures. Also they would record the transcriber's name, the person who bound the transcription, and the number of paper used (See Picture 1). Such kind of prefaces seemed like recorded archives. Scripture transcribers did not dare to be careless. So the transcribed scriptures in the early Tang Dynasty were of high quality.

In Tang Dynasty, there were official scripture

transcribers. Some of them did not only do transcriptions but also were responsible for the first round of proofreading. Even some of them were responsible for the second and third rounds of proofreading of their transcribed versions. This can be seen as self-supervision and inter-supervision of transcribers. Linghu Chongzhe, an official scripture transcriber of Xuanwu emperor of the Northern Wei Dynasty from Dunhuang County, was not only in charge of classics and scriptures but also was engaged in transcribing the Buddhist scriptures.

Just like imperial kilns and folk kilns in the ancient times, there were official transcription and individual transcription of scriptures. Some of the official scripture transcribers were official clerks and others were professional scripture transcribers. The Buddhist classic which was which was in the fifteenth year of the Chengping of the Northern Liang Dynasty (457) was transcribed by Fan Hai, an official clerk (See Picture 2). It was earlier than the fourteenth volume of *Satyasiddhi Shastra* in the Northern Wei Dynasty, which was signed by the official scripture transcriber. In Tang Dynasty, lots of official clerks were engaged in transcribing scriptures. Some of them were calligraphers who were familiar with all calligraphy schools and others were experts of regular script. And they would inform the administrations they were working for, such as the ministry of supervision and Central Secretariat. Transcriptions without mentioning of administrations indicated that the transcribers might be professional transcribers employed by the Buddhist temples. Individual transcribers were of different social status and some of them were from lower class. Zhu Changwen, a famous calligraphy theorist of the Northern Song Dynasty (960-1127), once wrote in his book about calligraphy theories that Wang Shaozong, a supervisor of Tang Dynasty had experiences about transcribing scriptures. So Zhu made conclusion that most of scripture transcribers in Tang Dynasty were officials. Actually, Wang Shaozong did not take an official ranking when he was engaged in transcribing and he once led a destitute life. According to the biography of Wang Shaozong, Wang was keen to learn and read when he was young and he read a lot of classics. He was specialized in cursive and clerical script. Living in a poor family, Wang was always employed by others to transcribe scriptures. After he got sufficient money to cover his living cost he refused any chance to transcribe even the payment was high. He lived in the temple and led a simple life for thirty years.

There once was a saying that transcribing scriptures was related to calligraphy. If the handwriting was good, the transcribed version would be widely spread among readers for years. Transcribing scripture was the profession of those transcribers. They took transcribing as their career, so they had to practice their handwriting. Therefore, transcribing scriptures could be regarded as something related to calligraphy. What the transcribers did was similar to the jobs of craftsmen. So there were certain standards for transcribers. Tao Hongjing of the Southern Dynasties (420-589) called it scripture calligraphy which was then called the calligraphy of scripture transcribers or the style of scripture transcription.

Before the *Dunhuang Transcribed Scriptures* came into being, the representative calligraphy of scripture transcription originated from Tang Dynasty. The calligraphy of scripture transcription which was popular in Song Dynasty (960-1279) mostly was that of people of Tang Dynasty. Since thousands volumes of the *Dunhuang Transcribed Scriptures* were found in the previous century, people became able to know about the calligraphy of scripture transcription from Jin Dynasty (265-420) to Tang Dynasty.

The calligraphy of scripture transcription in the Jin Dynasties and the Southern Dynasties was not as good as the handwriting style of Zhong Yao and Wang Xizhi, two distinguished calligraphers of Tang Dynasty whose handwriting were made copybooks for learning calligraphy among the superior at that time. Once Tao Hongjing discussed about the collection of calligraphy in the imperial storehouse with emperor Wu of Liang Dynasty, they talked about a lot of the calligraphy of scripture transcription. They agreed that the handwriting style of scripture transcription was just the copy of characters and the writing style was stereotyped without vitality. It can be concluded that the calligraphy of scripture transcribers was featured in this way. While transcribers took readers' feeling into account and they wrote in this way with the purpose of making the transcribed versions easy and clear for readers to read. And this was their standard code of writing (See Picture 3). Although the scripture transcribers were good at calligraphy, they could not write freely in their distinctive writing style like the officials and scholars. For scripture transcribers, the awareness of professional standard over-weighed the desire to practice their own writing style. From this perspective, calligraphy of scripture transcription differed from other style mainly because the era and the handwriting rather than different art of style of transcribers.

Before the sixth century, the calligraphy of scripture transcription in the northern area and scriptures (See Picture 4) looked more simple and rigid than the handwriting style of the southern area because the former one was isolated from the latter one. For example, the *heng* (horizontal stroke) began with sharpness and the end of this stroke was heavy. And the slant was something like *tiao* (right upward stroke). The structure of handwriting at that time kept more features of clerical script and it was similar to the calligraphy of scripture transcription of the Western Jin Dynasty (266-316). Calligraphy of the Western Jin Dynasty was similar to regular script and clerical script; however, they differed from regular and clerical scripts. Calligraphy of scripture transcription in the northern area after the sixth century changed a lot due to chinalization reform of the Northern Wei Dynasty. The calligraphy of the northern area assimilated features of calligraphy of the Southern Dynasties. The regular script of the Northern Wei Dynasty was the leading handwriting style, while the style changed from flatness to slant. However, compared with those renowned writings in regular script on the steles which were famous for their solidity and solemnity, the calligraphy of scripture transcription was not sophisticated and excellent. Handwriting works which are appreciated by calligraphers in modern time are those ones which were not included in the mainstream at that time. We can find some personal statements in the preface of transcribed scriptures of the Northern Dynasties (386-581), such like one transcriber said that he was assigned to transcribe the scriptures while his handwriting was not so good. A transcriber stated that he was not so specialized in handwriting while the other asked for forgiveness of his poor handwriting. There were other statements like these. Transcribing scripture demanded transcribers with high standard handwriting. However, when someone was in urgent need of transcription of scriptures for personal reasons, it might be hard for him to find an expert calligrapher as soon as he expected. Or people who were not rich enough to employ satisfying scripture transcribers could only find people with little knowledge about calligraphy to do the transcription. Hence, the standard of calligraphy of scripture transcription may differ from the actual handwriting of the transcribed scripture. The transcribed versions of scripture of the Northern Dynasties were almost the works of the unskilled transcribers. However, the perfect ones were the works of official clerks who took a job in the feudal government or someone who were once employed by the imperial institutions. These people got professional training of calligraphy. While they were so stereotyped by their own handwriting styles and they learned from the old-fashioned handwriting styles. So the calligraphy of scripture transcription of the Northern Dynasties was a little rigid and differed from various people.

In the Sui Dynasty (581-618), with the combination of handwriting in the southern area and the northern area, regular script stepped into a new stage. The scripture transcribers improved their handwriting skills. The plain and simple handwriting style and the primitive simplicity of handwriting in the Northern Dynasties were abandoned. By absorbing the handwriting style and skills of scripture transcribers in the Southern Dynasties, the calligraphy of the Northern Dynasties became brisk and simple.

Regular script of Tang Dynasty was famous for its

rules and regulations. There were so many distinguished calligraphers of Tang Dynasty, for example, Ouyang Xun was featured by rigidness. Yu Shinan was famous for his full and plump stroke. Chu Suiliang was known for his variation of handwriting. Yan Zhenqing was characterized by his solidity and powerfulness. Liu Gongquan specialized in elegance and strength. All these calligraphers were regarded as the standard and people followed example of them. Those scripture transcribers were deeply influenced by famous calligraphers. Their handwriting works were filled with fluent and precise strokes which were elegant and graceful. They stimulated the essence of handwriting of those calligraphers so that more and more transcriptions were made. During the years of the Xuanhe period of the Northern Song Dynasty, there was a transcribed version of the *Diamond Sutra* (also *Vajracchedika-sutra*) written by Tanlin (a religious scholar) in small regular script in the imperial storehouse. In the fifth volume of *Xuanhe Calligraphic Florilegium,* people remarked Tanlin's transcription like this: "All of its words adhered to one standard which made the text neat and regular so it was easy to read. Every stroke in it was with solidity and strength." According to this statement, it can be concluded that it was one of the best calligraphic works of scripture. There are many other transcribed versions which are as good as Tanlin's collected in the *Dunhuang Transcribed Scriptures*. Qian Yong, a famous calligrapher of the Qing Dynasty (1636-1912), praised scripture transcribers of the Tang Dynasty with whom people of the Song Dynasty and the Yuan Dynasty (1271-1368) could not compare.

People did not attach too much importance to the calligraphy of scripture transcription because the transcribers were from lower social class. Scholars and calligraphers looked down upon it because of its stereotype and sameness. All the transcribers conformed to the rules and regulations without their own styles and the works looked rigid. However, there were some experts in scripture transcription in the Tang Dynasty, whose handwriting were brisk with solid strokes. These transcribed versions in regular script surpassed the handwriting of regular script on the steles written by other famous calligraphers of the Tang Dynasty. If someone wants to learn regular script featured by people of the Tang Dynasty, he can follow the example of the best transcribed scripture. From the perspective of handwriting style and skill, these fantastic transcriptions will be easier to learn.

Calligraphy of scripture transcription of the two Jin Dynasties (265-420) and the Northern and Southern Dynasties was not featured by rigidness and elegance of those transcriptions of the Tang Dynasty which was difficult to follow. While it varied a lot in forms which made it impressive. Although these different forms of handwriting were not the outcomes of personality, they are now regarded as the inspiration of calligraphers in

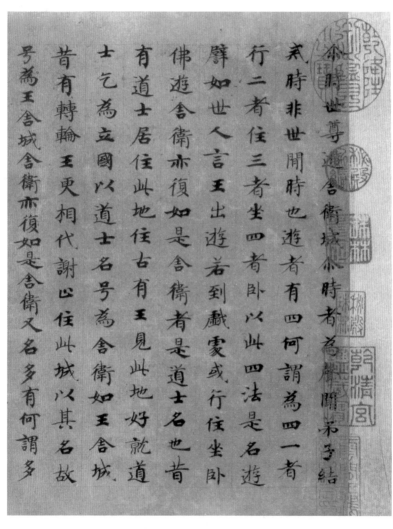

Guo Quan's transcribed *Shan-jian-lü* in Tang Dynasty(648, it once was collected in the imperial storehouse in the Southern Song Dynasty and Qing Dynasty, now it is collected in the Palace Museum, Beijing)

modern times.

The value of *Dunhuang Transcribed Scriptures* lies in it shows the improvement of regular script from the two Jin Dynasties to the Tang Dynasty. Researchers can find out many significant research subjects according to those different handwriting forms and skills. At least, the history of calligraphy in middle ancient times is colorful with various works of calligraphers rather than mono-performance of few renowned calligraphers.

We can find some transcribed versions of running script and cursive script in the *Dunhuang Transcribed Scriptures*. Some of the transcribed versions of cursive script are solid and fluent. Besides those famous works in cursive script such as those of Sun Guoting and Huaisu who were distinguished calligraphers of Tang Dynasty, there are also several excellent handwriting. So it can be concluded that cursive script was once very popular in the Tang Dynasty which is the significant resource for us to study calligraphy of the Tang Dynasty.

Calligraphy School and Doctors in Huizong Period

Liu Tao

In June 1104 (the third year of Chongning period of the Northern Song Dynasty, 960-1279), Emperor Zhao Zhe (1082-1135) set up calligraphy school, painting school and math school all of which belonged to Guozijian (the Imperial Academy). He also established the curriculums and examination mechanism for calligraphy school. Students in calligraphy school learnt seal script, clerical script and cursive script and mastered in ancient classics (*Shuowen, Zishuo, Erya, Boya* and *Fangyan*).

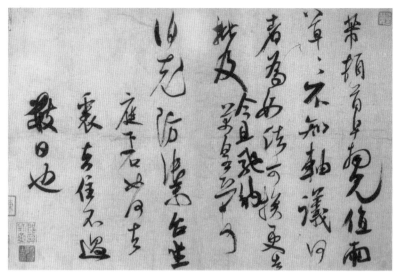

Mi Fu's *Zhiyu Tie* in Semi-cursive Script

There was no accurate number of calligraphy students in records, but it was said that this number was similar to the scale of math school, not more than 210.

Emperor Shenzong (1058-1085) issued *Xueling* in 1079 aiming at classifying calligraphy students into three grades: freshman (Wai Shesheng), junior (Nei Sheheng) and senior (Shang Shesheng). Freshmen took private exam per month and annual public exam. Those who ranked on the top two would upgrade to the junior. Every two years, the juniors took one examination to compete the top two grades so as to got the permission to be the senior. Senior students were also divided into three categories in accordance with their performance. We may conclude that even the best calligraphy students have to stay in the school at least for two years.

Calligraphy doctor referred to the teacher of calligraphy students. In the West Jin Dynasty (266-316), calligraphy doctor focused on skill-teaching. When it turned into the Tang Dynasty (618-907), calligraphy doctor started teaching ancient classics. Calligraphy doctor in the Song Dynasty(960-1279) taught both skills and ancient classics. Thus the whole mechanism of curricula was set up and called Shuxue (the academic calligraphy).

The development of calligraphy school went through ups and downs after its foundation. In 1106, for instance, schools of calligraphy, painting, math and medicine were deposed, while fifteen days later, three of them, except medical school were released. Similar case was also found in 1110. Then calligraphy school was affiliated to Guozijian (the Imperial Academy). However, the school was banned again in 1120, and freed in 1122.

Calligraphy school also experienced twists and turns in Huizong period, but history books didn't give the explanations. I guess maybe that the strict calligraphy-doctor-selecting mechanism should be to blame rather than lacking of students. Emperor Huizong was expert both in calligraphy and painting so that he was picky about selecting calligraphy doctors.

Mi Fu (1051-1107) was the most famous calligraphy doctor in the Huizong period. According to Cao Baoling (1946-)'s study, Mi Fu served as a calligraphy doctor between 1106 and 1107.Maybe his nomination on the calligraphy doctor was the reason that the once banned calligraphy school got released in the early of 1106.

There was another person in this position at the same time, named Li Shiyong. The twelfth volume of Xuanhe Pictures read that:

Li Shiyong was from Chengdu, Sichuan Province. His father and grandfather once served for the loyal family. All of them were famous for calligraphy. He was fond of writing poems and had a fine reputation in ink painting of bamboo.

The third volume of Heshan Inscription also mentioned Li Shiyong as a calligraphy doctor:

Two of his ink paintings of bamboo and three of his calligraphy works are masterpieces. He was the eldest son so that he called himself "Li Da".

Li Shiyong was famous for his paintings. He then started to learn calligraphy and beg books from Huang Tingjian, a famous calligrapher at that time. Huang spoke highly of him. Ten years later, Li Shiyong was promoted to be a calligraphy doctor.

The monument on which Li Shiyong depicted Emperor Huizong's script is located in the current Qian County, Shaanxi province. It was built in the eighth month of the second year of the Daguan period of the Northern Song Dynasty (1108). Li Shiyong's signature was easily identified on it. As a result, we may figure out that Li was still in the position of calligraphy doctor at that time.

Mi Youren, the eldest son of Mi Fu, was also in charge of calligraphy school. Yue Ke mentioned him in his book.

Mi Youren studied calligraphy and was in charge of calligraphy school for two years with Xu Jing and Du Tangji in the end of the Xuanhe period (1119-1125).

Xuanhe was the last reign mark of Emperor Huizong's reign, which lasted from 1119 to 1125. His inscription has Xu Jing's depictions written in 1147:

Calligraphy school was reset in 1122, the fourth year of the Xuanhe period. Tangji, Yuan Hui and Ji Yu were the three calligraphy doctors in the school. However Tangji died from political disaster (1126), Yuan Hui joined the army, and Ji Yu resigned.

Then, Mi Youren, Du Tangji and Xu Jing jointly took

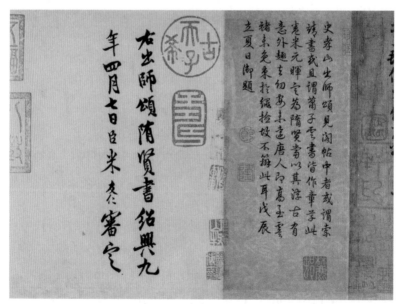

Mi Youren's Postcript to *Chushisong*

charge of the calligraphy school for two years. They were the last session under Emperor Huizong's ruling.

Now we could see some of Mi Youren's works, not only calligraphy works but also paintings.

Du Tangji died from political disaster. Emperor Zhao Gou (1107-1187) of the Southern Song Dynasty (1127-1279) once mentioned Du: Emperor Huizong loved calligraphy and made his mind to train calligraphers. Du Tangji was his only favorite. Du Tangji was the only calligraphy doctor who was educated and trained from the school. We could see that Du was highly praised by Emperor Zhao Gou. By then calligraphy school lasted for almost twenty years but only Du Tangji became well known after the school education. These showed the calligraphy school didn't meet its goals.

Xu Jing resigned between 1131 and 1162. He had a good reputation in seal script.

Calligraphy doctors could write all kinds of calligraphy. Li Shiyong, Mi Fu and Mi Youren were also famous for painting. At that time, ancient classics like *Shuowen, Erya, Fangyan,* and seal script were the common curricula both for painting school and calligraphy school. Calligraphy had a higher position than painting. As a result, calligraphy doctors are more famous than painting doctors, but they had to work harder. Some of calligraphy doctors even worked extremely hard. Nevertheless, they regarded these as an honor to please the emperor.

Su Shi and Calligraphy

We could say so much about Su Shi (1037-1101) in literature, painting, religion, or politics. Su Shi failed as a politician. Even though he was loyal to the emperor and the people, his comments on politics caused him many troubles, and he finally died very far away from home. He sacrificed his entire life in figuring out what is right or wrong in politics, but failed. His success in literature and arts only ranked after Li Bai (701-762) in the Tang Dynasty (618-907). He was regarded as the greatest

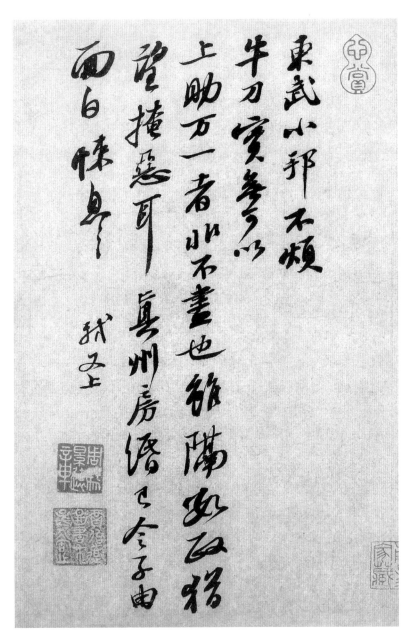

Su Shi's *Dongwu Tie* in running script (reserved in Taipei's Palace Museum, China)

writer in the Song Dynasty (960-1279) and had a talent in calligraphy as well. Although Cai Jing, the prime minister of the Song Dynasty, ordered to destroy Su's works, this could not prevent his works from spreading among the bottom dwellers. He was an honest person. Su Shi promoted his elder fellow Cai Xiang to be the top calligrapher of the Song Dynasty. However, Huang Tingjian (1045-1105) did not agree with him and regarded him as the crown calligrapher. It seemed like Huang was right because later generations saw Su Shi as one of Four Great Song Calligraphers.

Su Shi promoted *Yi* in calligraphy works

Su Shi mentioned character-writing many times in his poetry inscription. It seemed like he did not like the calligraphy law and really got sick of it. He stuck into *Yi* in calligraphy. He always said that his calligraphy style came from his heart rather than obeying any rules. Their later generation summarized their styles as *Yi* in priority, which may come from Su's view.

Calligraphers later than Wei and Jin dynasties (220-589), had always been confused by whether choosing to obey the rules or to *Yi*. Wang Xizhi (321-379) often used *Yi* to make comments on calligraphy works. In the early of Tang Dynasty, calligraphers advocated obeying the rules. When it came to Song Dynasty, Su Shi promoted Xie Yi.

Su Shi's *Luochi Shenmiao Stele* in regular script(carved in 1217, the tenth year of Jiading period in the Southern Song Dynasty)

He believed calligraphy-writing in accordance with his own mind was happy. As a result he wrote on his own will.

Three of the Four Great Song Calligraphers, Sushi, Huang Tingjian and Mi Fu (1051-1107), also promoted *Yi* in calligraphy. Su Shi did not work as hard as Huang Tingjian did in calligraphy nor paid as much patience as Huang Tingjian did to improve his calligraphy skill. Calligraphers in the later generations advocated hard-working stories from Zhang Zhi and Zhi Yong, but Su did not. His calligraphy skill came from his talent and knowledge. Huang Tingjian commented that Su was born to be a calligrapher just like Li Bai was born to be a poet. The picture shows how flying and lucid and brisk his calligraphy work is. Su said his calligraphy work was a combination of Cai Xiang, Yang Ningshi and Yan Fahua. Cai's works stuck into calligraphy rules. While Yang's work was bold and constrained. As for Yan, his work expressed bless and disaster.

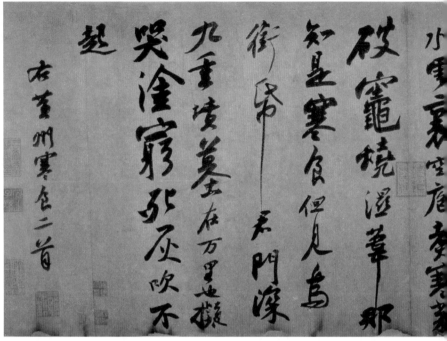

Su Shi's *Huangzhou Hanshi Tie* in running script (collected in Taipei's Palace Museum)

Su Shi hold the brush in a unique way, thus his calligraphy was quite different from the others. Huang Tingjian once said: "if we judge his calligraphy in accordance with the calligraphy rules, it would be easy to find out wrong writings." But Su Shi did not care so much about calligraphy rules which he believed of uniqueness.

Su Shi kept mentioning Yi when he talked about his calligraphy and relevant experiences. From his perspective, Yi had two meanings. On one hand, Yi represented calligraphers' characteristics and their psychological

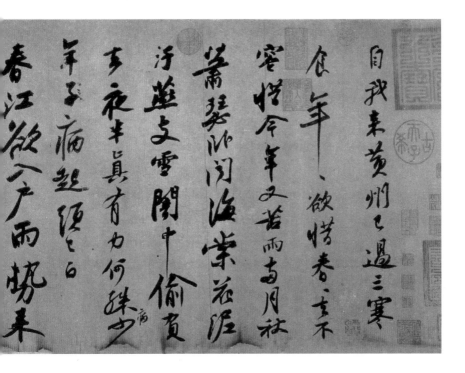

activities; on the other hand, individual calligraphy work expressed Yi. Yi was a coalition of calligrapher's heart and the calligraphy work. When the heart echoed with the calligraphy, one could achieve Yi. How to get Yi? Su explained that reading books as much as you can to set a solid foundation for Yi, then evaluated yourself to achieve Yi. We may find that a successful calligrapher must keep on acquiring knowledge and Yi like Su Shi did. Could this exemplify Su Shi's promotion of humanity in life?

Su Shi could write regular script, cursive script and running script. His famous cursive scripts Lin Wang

Youjun Jiang Tang Tie, Lin Heng Wenping Shu Tie and Meihua Shi Tie were collected in Xi Lou Su Tie by Wang Yingchen. Su Shi wrote cursive script when he was drunk. The original work Meihua Shi Tie showed the flying calligraphy. Regular script focused on rules which limited Su's Yi. Thus Su barely wrote regular script.

Su wrote running script extensively, because it barely limited his imagination. The style of running script set between regular script and cursive script. Calligrapher could write running script in his willing which may be the reason why Su preferred writing running script. He could set his own style in it. As a result Su's talent in calligraphy and success in art are commonly seen in his running scripts.

The most famous running script by Su Shi is the Poems Written at Huangzhou on the Cold Food Festival. It was regard as the No.3 running script in the world.

In February of 1080, 45-year-old Su Shi was demoted to Huangzhou (Huanggang, Hubei province) because of Wutai Poem Case. When he first landing at Huangzhou, there was no room for him. He had to stay at temple with monks. He finally got a small shabby room at Dongpo. In Huangzhou, he lived in a difficult situation but kept a positive attitude towards life.

The life in Huangzhou was the downturn of his political life but the peak of his art creation. He created so many poems in this period. The failure in politics disappointed him so much that he expressed his feeling through poems. When sending his calligraphy works to friends, he would ask them not to show his works to other people.

In the Spring of his third year in Huangzhou, he wrote three poems titled Poems at Huangzhou on Cold Food Festival to expressed his disappointment and described tough situation.

Su found only when writing could make him happy, so he expressed his feelings in his calligraphy works. Poems at Huangzhou on Cold Food Festival were his later works which showed his disappointments.

Before writing Poems at Huangzhou on Cold Food Festival, it seemed like he was in anxiety, which was showed in his calligraphy works.

The change of his emotion all expressed in his calligraphy works.

He wrote these poems without stopping. The variation of his words was quiet unique. His emotion flooded in the second poems through characters.

The first comment on the Poems written at Huangzhou on the Cold Food Festival came from Huang Tingjian who wrote that poems Su wrote were better than Li Bai, and the calligraphy wrote like the coalition from Yan Lugong, Yang Shaoshi and Li Xitai. From my point of view, these poems as his calligraphy works echoed with his heart, and finely express Xie Yi. these could be the reason why the Poems Written at Huangzhou on the Cold Food Festival stands on the top among his rest works.

Feibai Script

There is no evidence proving who first wrote the feibai script, but Ciyuan connected it to Cai Yong (133-192). Ciyuan explained that feibai script was a style of calligraphy characterized by hollow strokes, as if done with a half-dry brush.

It made sense to regard Cai Yong as the founder of feibai script for two reasons. Firstly, feibai script originated in the period when Cai lived in. Then feibai script was

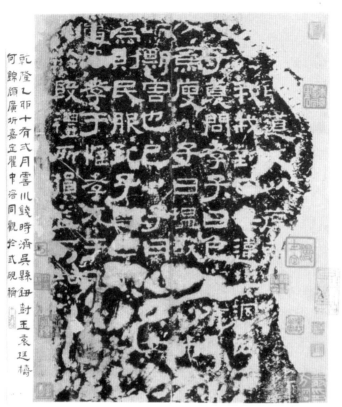

Xiping Shijing by Cai Yong

welcomed by other calligraphers who hereby tended to connect it to the celebrity like Cai Yong.

Feibai script was believed appeared in the period when Cai Yong lived in for following reasons: feibai script got popular in the period when Cai lived. According the historical references, two calligraphers who were good at feibai script in the Han dynasty (25-220) were Cai Yong and Zhang Zhi. The first book theoretically talked about feibai script was Feibai Xu Shi, written by Zhang Hong in the Three Kingdoms Period (220-280) which was later than Han Dynasty. Theory always comes later than pragmatic works.

Some facts show that calligraphers attached great importance to feibai script. There were much books talking about feibai script. Many famous calligraphers and emperors, such as Wang Xizhi (321-379) and Wang Xianzhi (344-386), both famous calligraphers and Emperor Li Shimin (598-649) and Empress Wu Zetian (624-705) of the Tang Dynasty (618-907), also wrote feibai script. The loyal family took measures to generalize feibai script. And Empress Wu Zetian even selected one calligraphy doctor to teach feibai script at loyal school.

Feibai script was popular for some time, but finally faded away. Lu Shaozeng and Zhang Yanchang co-edited Feibai Catalog on calligraphers in all dynasties.

There were not so many calligraphers who specialized in feibai script from every dynasty, and this number kept shrinking. Some of the most famous calligraphers before the Tang Dynasty specialized in feibai script, while none of the most famous calligraphers in the Song Dynasty (960-1279) could write feibai script. Because feibai scripts were not welcomed by calligraphy connoisseurs. So what caused the decline of the once popular feibai script?

Wang Xizhi once praised feibai script for its Yi. Yi

represents the core value of calligraphy art. Feibai script also had Yi, so what is the Yi of feibai script?

In fact, Yi of feibai script was expressed by fei and bai. They represented different kinds of beauty. Fei stood for the beauty in "Shi", while "bai" was on behalf of the beauty of light.

Aesthetics regards "shi" as a dynamic illusion which might have certain influence on viewers. Let's go deeper. "Shi" could be the life in miniature, because life is dynamic. Feibai script shows a flying gesture. As for feibai's origin in calligraphy, it came from Bafen style to which a flying gesture was important. Thus, a flying gesture in feibai script was called the beauty in"shi".

Due to the special brush adopted in feibai-script writing, characters are looked like written by half-dry wood. This uniqueness raised attentions. "Bai" referred to the blankness which present lightness. And lightness comes from the application of light. Thus the essence of 'bai' is to perfectly maneuvering the light. Many ancient artists including calligraphers attached great importance to the application of light. It also made sense to the light for Apollo, the god of sun in ancient Greek arts. As a result, "bai"of feibai script represented the beauty of light.

The coalition of the beauty of shi and light created a beauty of flying lightness which was the main sector of Yi in terms of feibai script. However it could not prevent feibai script from declining.

Ye Lang (1938-) believed the creation of art (including calligraphy) equaled to the creation of Yixiang. Yixiang came from the core spirit of nature (Ye Lang, *Outline of Chinese Aesthetics History*). It was relevant to Daoism. Yixiang formed the beauty of calligraphy. Even though the flying lightness of feibai script originated from nature, it is far away from the core value of Yixiang. That may explain much.

The creation of Yixiang began with shaping different lines. Li Zehou (1930-) illustrated the art of lines was the lines that vivid, flowing, fresh, and really beautiful. That is the Chinese calligraphy (Li Zehou, *The Path of Beauty*). On the contrary, feibai script advocated a systematic rule in writing so that it lacked of expressiveness. What's more, the flying and light lines of feibai script only in a single style cannot bear closer analysis.

Different lines formed the changing characters which set a solid foundation for achieving the beauty of light. Black lines and white space between different lines varied. As a result, the beauty of light was endless. Clearly this kind of beauty cannot be reached by feibai script.

With the beauty both in 'shi' and in light, feibai script once got its popularity. With the development calligraphy, the essence of the calligraphy art came to clearer and the aesthetic ideal of calligraphy was highlighted while the aesthetic value of feibai script was shaded. The decline of this script could not be avoided. When it came to the Qing

Dynasty, calligraphers even regarded feibai script as the poorest script forms. While this ideal may sound arbitrary.

By the way, there was a time when calligraphy scripts flourished. Wang Yin edited thirty-six kinds of scripts including feibai script in Northern Dynasty (386-581). So did Wei Xu. He catalogued fifty-six kinds of scripts also including feibai script in Tang Dynasty, among which apart from seal script, official script, regular script, running script and cursive script, all ended like feibai script. Although they ended for different reason, we cannot ignore the common one—lower status in aesthetics.

The Wildness of Wild Cursive Script

Wild cursive script is an art form which is the most wild and unrestrained one in the system of cursive script. Some works of Zhang Xu and Huaisu, two famous calligraphers of the Tang Dynasty (618-907), are the representatives of the wild cursive script school. Before the midterm of the Tang Dynasty, people who learned cursive script held Wang Xizhi and Wang Xianzhi's modern cursive script as standard. Generation after generation, people regarded this standard as rules and regulations. In

Handwriting in cursive script of Zhang Xu

the midterm of the Tang Dynasty, representatives of cursive script calligraphers such as Zhang Xu and Huaisu, did something different and they neglected the previous standard. They regarded handwriting of cursive script as means for venting and leading off their emotions. And their handwriting showed the feature of wildness and unrestraint of cursive script as much as possible. In *The New Book of Tang,* a book introduces history of the Tang Dynasty, there were statements about Zhang Xu, it was said that Zhang Xu was a kind of alcoholic, and he wrote in a wild and unrestrained way when he got drunk. When he got awake, he had a look of his handwriting and he was also surprised by his work. People at that time called him Zhang Dian (Dian, a Chinese word means craziness). In one of Huaisu's works, there was a quotation saying that people called Zhang Xu as Zhang Dian because of his handwriting and Huaisu was once called a crazy man because of his wildness and unrestraint of handwriting. Zhang Xu and Huaisu were both representatives of the new form of cursive script. Since then, the wild cursive script came into being.

Though Zhang Xu and Huaisu had made their handwriting in the way of wild cursive script at that time, the name of wild cursive script did not come up until the Ming Dynasty (1368-1644). The handwriting style of Zhang Xu and Huaisu, together with others' imitation of their handwriting style, were called wild cursive script for the first time. Zhao Yiguang, a scholar of the Ming Dynasty, wrote in his book that works of Zhang Zhi, Zhang Xu and Huaisu were of wild cursive script. Their works are all included in the system of cursive script while each of them varies a lot with others. The works of wild cursive script of Zhang Zhi can be regarded as the fake, which is analyzed in details in books of scholars of the Northern Song Dynasty (960-1127) and the Qing Dynasty (1636-1912). Lou Jian, a scholar of the Ming Dynasty, once stated that Zhang Xu and Huaisu were famous for their wild cursive script handwriting. Wang Shizhen, an official of the Ming Dynasty (1368-1644) said that Zhang Xu and Huaisu were supposed to be the originators of wild cursive script. It was not accident that the name of wild cursive script came into being during the Ming Dynasty. There used to be lots of calligraphers whose handwriting were of wild cursive script style and their works were widely spread. Because of the popularity of wild cursive script at that time, people had to name this kind of new form of handwriting.

Based on how people gave the name to wild cursive script and how people used the name, it can be concluded that people regarded it as another form of cursive script, such as *zhangcao* (early form of cursive script which is based on clerical scrip) and modern cursive script. Nowadays, people still hold this opinion toward wild cursive script. For example, Jiang Shanguo, an expert of Chinese character, once pointed out in his book that, there are totally three forms of cursive script: the early form of cursive script, the modern cursive script and the wild cursive script. Zhong Mingshan, a calligrapher in modern times, he said that cursive script includes early form of cursive script, modern cursive script and wild cursive script.

Is it possible to regard wild cursive script as a parallel form of early form of cursive script and modern cursive script? The answer is not so clear. Being the subsidiary handwriting style, the early form of cursive script is the counterpart of clerical script while the modern cursive script is that of regular script. Since clerical script and regular script are parallel, correspondingly, the early form of cursive script and the modern cursive script can be parallel. Judging from the forming process of wild cursive script, there is not a symbol system of wild cursive script which represents the contents of it and there are no fixed criteria of measurement of its degree of illegibility. Actually, wild cursive script originated from the modern cursive script. Superficially, the counterpart of wild cursive script is regular script. However, there is no direct relationship between these two. Wild cursive script originated from the modern cursive script whose counterpart is regular script. There are so many differences between wild cursive script and modern cursive script. So we cannot parallel wild cursive script with the modern cursive script. Therefore, wild cursive script also cannot be paralleled with the early form of cursive script.

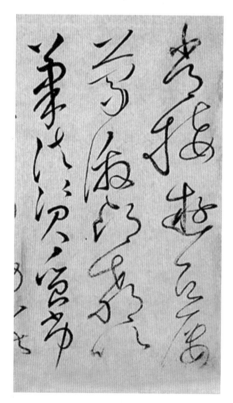

Handwriting in cursive script of Huaisu

Wild cursive script cannot be paralleled with the early form of cursive script and modern script. What's more, it is not even a style of calligraphy. Wildness, the word itself means unruliness and indiscipline, which can be used to describe certain kind of handwriting style. In the pursuit of calligraphy style, all styles of calligraphy include two different presentations: the one with wildness, while the other without wildness. Wild cursive script can include these two presentations if we recognize it as a kind of handwriting style. However, there will be a paradox, that is, dose the wild cursive script without wildness belong to wide cursive script? So, wild cursive script itself will be a controversial problem if we take it as a style of calligraphy.

In fact, wild cursive script, as a special form of modern cursive script, is about individual expression on the basis of modern cursive script. While from the perspective of the study of character, wild cursive script does not have its own characteristics. Liu Xizai, a literary theorist of the Qing Dynasty, once wrote some statements of cursive script in his book, *General Introduction of Calligraphy*. Liu wrote in his book that, Sun Guoting, a calligraphy theorist gave an evaluation of Wang Xizhi's handwriting: without sharpness. Du Fu, a distinguished poet of the Tang Dynasty, remarked Zhang Xu's handwriting as wildness and unruliness. The former one is like motionless water while the latter is like running water. Wild cursive script is just like running liquid while the modern cursive script is more like motionless water. Differences between them are just at superficial level, the symbol system inside them is similar. Comparing with the modern cursive script, wild cursive script expresses more in an aesthetic way. It is no exaggeration that wild cursive script is a form of art for appreciation. That is to say, wild cursive script is an artistic form of cursive script rather than a style of calligraphy from the perspective of the study of character.

Wild cursive script is an art form of cursive script which is featured by wildness rather than a style of calligraphy. So, how can we define the word "wildness"? This article argues that the key of wildness means surpassing. To be specific, wild cursive script surpasses in two different aspects. At first, judging from the form, wildness of wild cursive script is featured by impressive visual impact which surpasses general cursive script in the aspect of artistic style.

Impressive visual impact of cursive script is the wildness of the pattern and form of characters. The wildness of characters' pattern results from comparison. Some of the characters are especially big while others are so small. Some strokes are so strengthened while the others are so mild. There are also contrasts in other aspects, for instance, angled and round turns, curvy and straight lines, and deficiency and excess of strokes. Wildness of form of characters is mainly caused by various tendencies. Some people write in a flat way while others write in a contracted way. Some people remain a simple style while others change their styles all the time.

Liu Xizai wrote in his book, there are wild seal script and wild clerical script, as well as elegant running script and elegant cursive script. The latter is not only elegant but also wild. Wildness contrasts with elegance. Elegance means standard. Standard means formal condition. Wildness means strange which leads to extraordinary. So wildness means surpassing standard. Cai Xizong, a calligrapher of the Tang Dynasty, said in his book, *On Calligraphy,* Zhang Xu's handwriting was creative and extraordinary with his imagination, which broke the old rules in some ways. Wang Xizhi's handwriting was much simpler and contracted. All characters in Wang's works were wild and unrestrained. Ren Hua, a literary scholar of the Tang Dynasty, wrote in his book, that the sage of cursive script was well-known. Calligraphy works of Wang Xizhi and Wang Xianzhi were famous for splendor but lack of some wild strokes. Zhang Xu was unique and unruly. Ren Hua said Huaisu was a talent who was characterized by wildness and unruliness. Talking about Zhang Xu's extraordinary handwriting, it is exactly the visual impact of his cursive script which makes him unique and outstanding. Huaisu's wildness makes him different. All of their handwriting styles surpass the traditional art form and make them extraordinary.

Wei Dynasty, Zhong Yao, *Xuan-shi-biao*,
imitated version in National Library of China
(partial)

We cannot ignore the fact that wildness of calligraphy means surpassing traditional cursive script. However, the transformation is not casual and random, but depends on the pursuit of beauty of calligraphy. Liu Xizai once said in his book, *General Introduction of Calligraphy*, that Zhang Xu and Huaisu hold a serious attitude towards their handwriting. They did not learn from the superficial perspectives. They absorbed other's strengths and made their own efforts. If calligraphers overlook the aesthetic quality of wildness and consider wildness as complete unruliness, they will fail to create those excellent works.

Secondly, from the perspective of content, wildness is free externalization of the calligrapher's spirit, a kind of improvement of personality.

The form co-exists with the content. The wildness of pattern and form of characters can be achieved, and spiritual components of the calligraphers play a much more important role in this process than a certain formula of calligraphy. Zhang Huaiguan, a calligrapher and a calligraphy theorist of the Tang Dynasty, once said that there were differences between cursive script and regular script. As for regular script, the content ends up with the character. The handwriting of cursive script seems to be everlasting. Lots of components are included in the cursive script. The pattern of characters can be seen as a combination of the characters and feelings of the calligrapher, including his ambition or his frustration.

Liu Xizai, in his opinion, other styles of calligraphy focus on the rules and regulations while cursive script attach more importance to meanings and contents which were carried by the characters. People who are unfamiliar with cursive script may be not able to express his ideas due to the restricted rules of handwriting. While if a person is good at cursive script, he can make perfect combination of the rules and his expression, which means that he can express his thoughts by writing in a wild and unrestrained way. Zhang Zhiping, a scholar of the Qing Dynasty, stated that among the four styles of calligraphy, seal script, clerical script, regular script and cursive script, cursive script is the most difficult one. The other three styles of calligraphy have the track of stokes while cursive script is so changeable that there is no specified track of strokes. Cursive script, without specified rules for strokes, changes all the time with the variation of the calligrapher's spirit. Although some people were good at cursive script, sometimes it is difficult for them to make an end of their handwriting. If these people were intended to do something, they could not make out excellent works. Unlike other styles of calligraphy with certain standard, people can create their calligraphy works in their own way. Cursive script focuses much on the meaning and content which are seen as the externalization of the calligrapher's spirit. Calligraphers would do worse if they are deliberate to concentrate on the meaning and content. Based upon general cursive script, wild cursive script stresses much more on the calligraphers' spirit and idea. Wildness, the word itself is used to describe a concept which is related to spirit. Wild cursive script stresses on the meaning and content of the characters. And the rules of handwriting, which are invisible, are mixed with that. If the rules overweigh the meaning and content, then the work is not a good one. While if the rules surpass a lot, it means that the calligraphers are intended to show off their skills of calligraphy.

As for the creation of wild cursive script, there is only one way which is feasible, that is to allow spirit vary freely. From the perspective of psychology, spirit includes recognition, emotion, intention, and others. Talking about the creation of wild cursive script, individual spirit includes the outcome of aesthetic training, aesthetic attitude and will, and conditions of emotion. Han Yu, a literary scholar of the Tang Dynasty, wrote some sentences in his book to describe Zhang Xu. Han said that Zhang Xu was fond of cursive script and almost did not have any other hobbies. Zhang Xu regarded writing in the style of cursive script as a way out of all kinds of his emotions, for instance, happiness and sadness, worry and sympathy, complaint, admiration, and other feelings. All of these natural phenomena, including the splendid landscape and scenery, lively animals, beautiful flowers, the earth and the moon, and wind and rain, are source of inspiration of Zhang Xu's creation of his handwriting. Therefore, Zhang Xu's handwriting is easily changeable and unruly. Zhang Xu's handwriting works were not restrained in a specified standard. He used his handwriting to express his intentions and ideas. So his wild cursive script naturally became the external presentation of his spirit.

It should be noted that the externalization of spirit happens on specific conditions. All of people are included in certain social network. Therefore, inevitably, we take our own interests into consideration. Apart from that, we will be influenced by a psychological system of self-evaluation. Hence, there are always restrictions in the process of the creation of calligraphy, which makes it difficult to achieve the externalization of spirit. Generally speaking, creation of calligraphy is a rational behavior which is less influenced by those restrictions. Since being rational is a kind of restriction. Changeable spirit plays a significant role in the process of cursive script creation which focuses on spirit. Being rational plays a less important role. Calligraphers must get rid of all kinds of restrictions while the intention to eliminate restrictions is another kind of obstacle. That's why people say that the style of cursive script is difficult especially wild cursive script. Even if there are difficulties in the creation process, Zhang Xu made it, expressing all of his ideas and thoughts by writing in the style of wild cursive script. Also Huaisu did that. Once there were poets wrote poems about Huaisu, saying that Huaisu did successfully get rid of restrictions when he created his handwriting. Huaisu's success implied that the absence of being rational and restriction of his creation. He made free externalization of his spirit. In some way, free externalization of spirit means the calligraphers should get rid of all kinds of restrictions that may affect their creations completely so that they can behave beyond the ordinary personality. According to the scholars' remarks on Zhang Xu and Huaisu, it can be concluded that they surpass themselves when they did creation of wild cursive script.

As it is mentioned above, wild cursive script got its name during the Ming Dynasty due to its great popularity. Can we conclude that it is not so difficult to learn wild cursive script and get the essence of it?

There once were lots of calligraphers of the Ming Dynasty who were said to be specialized in wild cursive script. However, is the so-called wild cursive script the real one? Judging from the form, lots of calligraphy works of wild cursive script at that time were not wild in the aspects of the style and pattern of calligraphy. The wildness and unruliness of wild cursive script cannot be eliminated. Without the feature of wildness, the wild cursive script cannot bear its name. Judging from the content, calligraphy works at that time were restrained in some ways. Calligraphers seemed to manage to remain and imitate the wildness without their own creation, which seemed like a mechanical creation. Wild cursive script like this can be seen as the fake cursive script. Some literary scholars of the Ming Dynasty once criticized those calligraphers of wild cursive script. The literary scholars pointed out that these calligraphers did not get the essence of wild cursive script. Xie Jin, Zhang Bi and Ma Yilong were renowned calligraphers of cursive script in the Ming Dynasty. However, their calligraphy works cannot be seen as the real wild cursive script. Generally speaking, all of those calligraphy works of the Ming Dynasty were not the real form of wild cursive script. Talking about reasons for this phenomenon, environment of the era plays an important role. Apart from this, how did people recognize wild cursive script is another factor. Calligraphers of the Ming Dynasty regarded wild cursive script as a style of calligraphy without the realization that it is actually an art form. They did not realize the fact that wild cursive script was an improvement of the art form. Some of them believed that they can learn about it, while others tried every effort to imitate it. Finally, wild cursive script of the Ming Dynasty became very strange, without the essence of real wild cursive script.

Chinese calligraphy has developed into an independent art form since the late Han Dynasty (25-220) and the Three Kingdoms period (220-280). In the Eastern Jin Dynasty (317-420), calligraphy became a fashion in the upper class and people would compete for the best calligraphers. Finally Wang Xizhi, "Sage of Calligraphy", appeared. He was known to be one of the most esteemed Chinese calligraphers of all time and a master of all forms of Chinese calligraphy. Besides, he was also an excellent representative of the Chinese cultural history.

Wang Xizhi (321-379, or 303-361), style name (*zi*) Yishao, courtesy name (*hao*) Danzhai, was a native of Langya (now Linyi, in Shandong) and later moved to Shanyin, Kuaiji (now Shaoxing, in Zhejiang). During his career, he held various official positions: Imperial Secretary (in charge of books and documents), Military Staff Officer, Administrator of Kuaiji, and General of the Right Army. So he was also called "Wang Youjun" (literally General of the Right Army).

Wang Xizhi was born into a noble family. His uncles Wang Dao, Wang Dun, and his father Wang Kuang were all influential ministers of the Eastern Jin Dynasty. Wang Xizhi was very upright and insightful. One day when he was young, Chijian (a supreme government official in charge of military affairs) came to his home to choose a son-in-law. Everyone was very nervous on the news except for him, who was still lying in bed eating with his belly naked, showing his special temperament. He once offered important and practical political opinions to the Prime Minister Xie An and an official called Yin Hao. When he was governor of Kuaiji, he made great efforts to save the hungry people by "distributing imperial grain" and "cutting off wine supplies for a year". It demonstrated that he was a man with political ambition and a compassionate heart for the public. But after frequent setbacks in politics, he had to follow the Confucian teaching "troubled, improve yourself; valued, improve the world", turned to mountains and woods for a simple and pleasant life, and studied calligraphy. Of course, influenced by the values and fashions of his age and society, he also had the habit of "fushi" (a cultivation method of Taoism), "qingtan" (repeated discussion on metaphysics problems), and paid great attention to appearances like most scholar-bureaucrats of the Wei and Jin Dynasties. But different from those rich men who did nothing, he focused on calligraphy, through which his personal character and ambitions were fully demonstrated.

Wang Xizhi began to learn calligraphy at seven. He secretly read his father's books on calligraphy at twelve, and then was taught by his uncle Wang Yi and Wei Shuo (Lady Wei), offspring of calligraphers Wei Ji and Wei Guan. Wang Yi and Wei Shuo were taught by Zhong Yao who was proficient in *kaishu* (the regular script). So Wang Xizhi gained the merits of Zhong Yao's calligraphy. Later he learnt calligraphy directly from famous calligraphers and well-known steles. Learning widely, he ended up as a master of all writing styles. But he made bold innovations rather than stick to the classical rules. He wrote the sentence "All things in the world have their own features but what I love is something fresh and creative", kind of his motto, when he was at the Orchid Pavilion for the purification rites of spring. After a long time of great

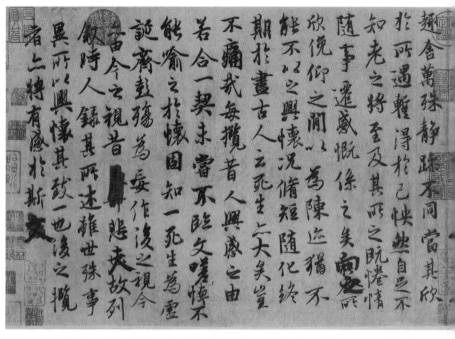

Shenlong's Edition of *Orchid Pavilion* (Collected in the Palace Museum, Beijing)

efforts, he finally created a brand-new *kaishu* system in his old ages. If the *kaishu* of Zhong Yao was still shadowed by *lishu* (the clerical script), the handwriting of Wang Xizhi basically got rid of the influence of *lishu*. He formed a style of flowing grace, creating a new age of calligraphy.

It is difficult to cover all the Wang Xizhi's achievements in calligraphy in the short essay. But I will talk about it briefly in the following aspects.

1. Forceful and powerful. Chinese calligraphy calls for force of hands, because force is believed to be an important element of the beauty of calligraphy. Lady Wei once said

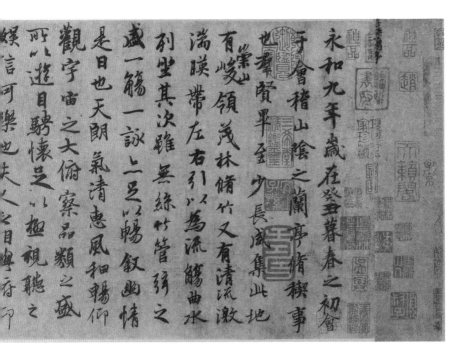

that force gave calligraphy life. Wang Xizhi's writing is famous for his force. Emperor Wu of Liang (Xiao Yan, ruling from 502-549) spoke highly of Wang's calligraphy and praised his amazing force. Here is a story of Wang Xizhi. He wrote on the wooden floor and wanted to erase the writings after finishing. But the writings still remained even after he had took off three *fen* (three *fen* equals one centimeter) of the wood. This is the origin of the idiom "ru mu san fen", which refers to forceful handwritings.

2. Flexible and natural. People were no longer satisfied with the invariable *Guange* style (an official writing

style: square and serious) after calligraphy became an art. They believed that the best calligraphy should be flexible in writing technique, style and structure. Wang Xizhi's writing demonstrated perfect flexibility, which was acknowledged by later generations. Such flexibility could be seen in *Supplementary Biography* and *Guang chuan shu ba,* and even from the praise of Emperor Taizong of Tang (ruling from 626-649). It is true that Wang's writings vary in font size and line spacing. Even the blank space was arranged elaborately. The Chinese character "zhi" appeared more than 20 times in *Lanting Xu* (Preface to the Poems Collected from the Orchid Pavilion) but each was in a unique style. In addition, each stroke of the characters in *Chu yue tie* (A Letter Beginning with "Lunar January") was unique. It was no wonder that Sun Guoting said Wang's writings were full of changes. All the changes and arranges were incredibly natural.

3. Free and graceful. The beauty of calligraphic art is not restricted to calligraphic forms (like writing technique, style, and structure). More importantly it can reflect the attributes of the calligrapher and his society through forms, such as a person's character, cultivation, virtue, artistic ideal, and the spirit of the times. Wang Xizhi's writing was graceful yet natural, brisk yet solemn, serious yet leisurely, free yet forceful. It can be proven by the social reality, his ideological tendencies, and personality traits. *A New Account of the Tales of the World* described Wang

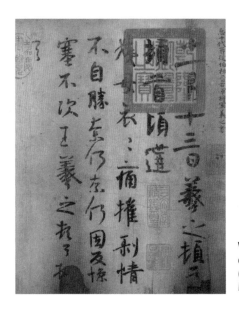

Wang Xizhi's early semi-cursive script *Yimu* (Collected in Liaoning Museum)

Xizhi as unrestricted and special. Yuan Ang of the Liang Dynasty (502-557) said that his writing was like that of the Xie family, unrestricted and natural. The calligraphy theorist Liu Xizai of the Qing Dynasty (1616-1911) made a more detailed analysis of his calligraphy and said, "The personality of Wang Xizhi could be shown when Xi Jian came to his home to choose a son-in-law. He was lying in bed with his belly naked and cared nothing about the incident, just like the quietness and calmness of his writing. His statecraft could be seen when he advised Xie An to be practical and realistic in government affairs, just like the pragmatic nature of his writing." The master of calligrapher with skillful techniques could not only reflect stable temperament and character traits but also integrate

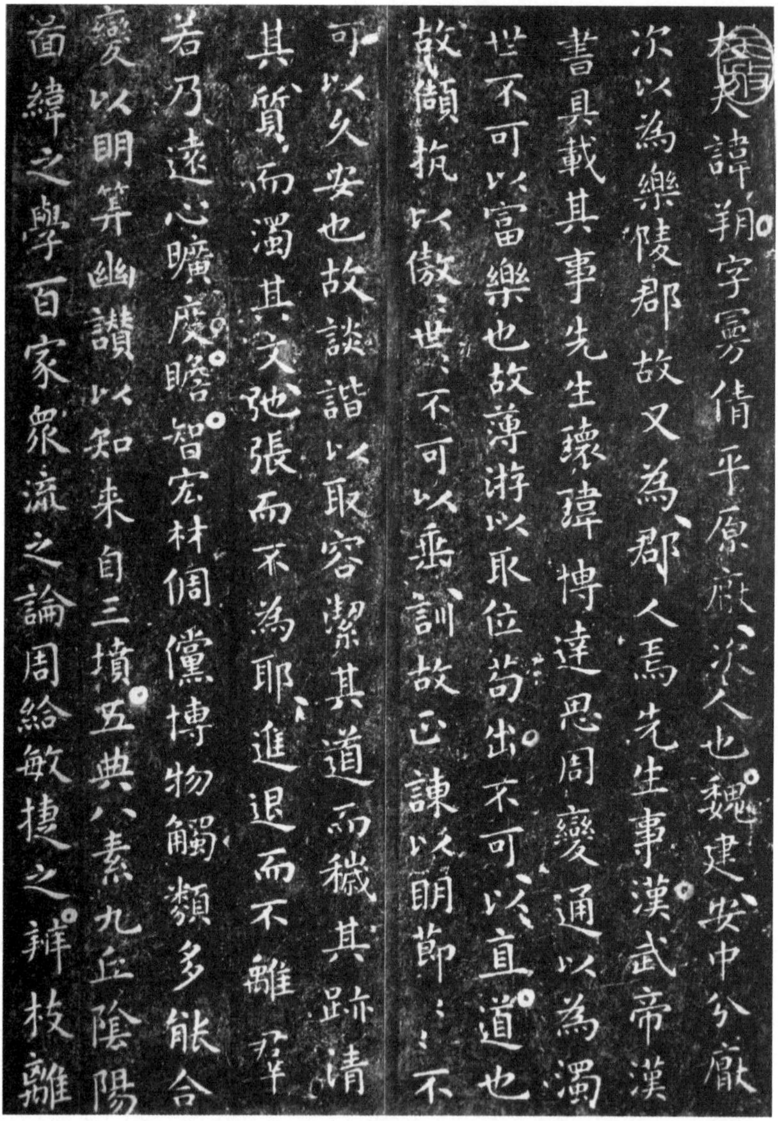

圖緯之學百家眾流之論周給敏捷之辯枝枚離

若乃遠心曠度瞻智宏材倜儻博物觸類多能合　變以明算讚以知來自三墳五典八素九丘陰陽

其質而濁其文弛張而不為耶進退而不離　可以久安也故談諧以取容潔其道而穢其跡清

故頡頏以傲世不可以垂訓故正諫以明節　不

世不可以富樂也故薄游以取位苟出不可以直道也

書具載其事先生瓌瑋博達思周變通以為濁

次以為樂陵郡故又為郡人焉先生事漢武帝漢

讚朔字曼倩平原厭次人也魏建安中分厭

Wang Xizhi's regular script *On Portrait of Dongfang Shuo*

88

his emotions into writing, as was proven by *Treatise of Calligraphy* of Sun Guoting.

Wang Xizhi's skillful and changeable writing style, together with his great cultural accomplishment, special thoughts and characters, and implicit expression makes his handwriting difficult to appreciate or learn. Zhang Huaiguan once said that "He shows little so people find it difficult to learn; he conveys deep so few people can understand". If we just learn his handwriting without knowing his background or character, we may end up like Zhao Mengfu whose writing seems like that of Wang's, regular and nice, but less forceful, changeable or meaningful. This is what we should pay attention to.

None of Wang Xizhi's original handwriting has survived, but there are a number of copies, such as *Yimu* (A Letter Expressing Sorrow on Aunt's Death), *Chu yue* (A Letter Beginning with "Lunar January"), *Sang luan* (A Letter Expressing Great Anguish), *Shangyu* (A Letter Written in Shangyu), and *Lanting Xu* (Preface to the Poems Collected from the Orchid Pavilion). The ancient rubbings include *Huangting*, *Yueyi*, and *Shi qi tie* (A Long Scroll of Letters Beginning with "Seventeen"). As to steles, *Sheng Jiao xu* (Introduction to the Sacred Teachings of Monk Tripitaka of the Great Tang Dynasty) collected by Huairen is the most famous.

Draft of a Requiem to My Nephew by Yan Zhenqing

Wang Yuchi

Yan Zhenqing is famous as a loyal martyr in history. Along the development of Chinese calligraphy, he is the most influential calligrapher after Wang Xizhi. Su Shi spoke highly of his *Yan* style and even said that "Du Zimei's poetry and Yan Lugong's calligraphy were peerless throughout history". Yan Zhenqing's *Draft of a Requiem to My Nephew* is known as "the best *Yan* writings (calligraphy) ever" and "the second best *xingshu* (semi-

90

cursive script) in China" (the best is *Lanting XU* by Wang Xizhi). Indeed, among the remaining *Yan* writings, *Draft of a Requiem to My Nephew* has typical meanings in both contents and calligraphic art.

Draft of a Requiem to My Nephew was written in 758 (during the reign of Emperor Suzong of Tang). We can see from the title that it is a requiem draft in memory of his late nephew Yan Jiming. With more than 200 Chinese characters, it briefly recorded the stories of Jiming and his father Yan Gaoqing (Yan Zhenqing's cousin), including their counter-insurgency, getting killed and relatives looking for the bodies.

Yan Zhenqing (709-785), with a style name (*zi*) of Qingchen, was a native of Langya (now Linyi, in Shandong) and born in Wannian, Jingzhao (now Xi'an, in Shaanxi). He was once Governor of Pingyuan, Minister of Law, and princes' private tutor. He was conferred the title of Duke of Lu. In 753 when he was Investigating Censor, he was marginalized by Yang Guozhong and sent out of the capital as the governor of Pingyuan (now Dezhou, in Shandong). An Lushan, the military commissioner of Pingyuan, was to rebel and Yan noticed it. So Yan sent emergency memorial to the emperor and started to prepare for war by fortifying the city wall and stocking up provisions. In 755, An Lushan and Shi Siming rebelled. The ill-prepared Tang government troops retreated with little resistance from most northern prefectures; only Yan

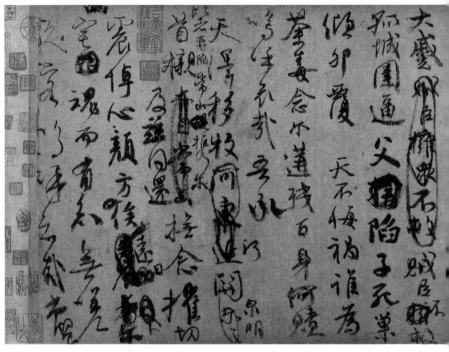

Draft of a Requiem to My Nephew by Yan Zhenqing

Zhenqing's Pingyuan sustained through. Being loyal, Yan was supported by a lot of people from all directions and selected leader of the troop guarding the emperor. Yan Gaoqing, Governor of Changshan (now Gaocheng, in Hebei), combined force with Yan Zhenqing and fought against the rebels at the rear. Yan Jiming helped them keep in contact. Yan Gaoqing managed to kill Li Qincou, an adherent of An Lushan who was guarding Tumen (now Jingxing, in Hebei), and occupied the strategic place. He sent his eldest son Yan Quanming to escort

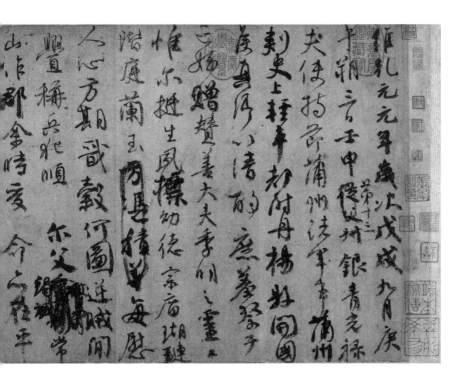

captives to Chang'an to report the victory and ask for help. Unexpectedly, when they arrived at Taiyuan, they were intercepted by Wang Chengye, the military commissioner of Taiyuan. Wang rewrote the memorial to the throne, made the exploits his own and even resisted to help. Knowing the accident in Hebei, An Lushan besieged Changshan. After three days of fierce fight, food and water in Changshan began to run out. Changshan fell into the hands of enemies and Gaoqing was captured. Rebels threatened Gaoqing to surrender by putting a knife on his son (Jiming)'s head. But Gaoqing did not give in and Jiming's head was cut off. Then rebels tied Gaoqing to a bridge in Luoyang, cut off his foot and killed him by dismemberment. Later Yan Zhenqing sent Quanming to look for the bodies of Gaoqing and Jiming in Luoyang and Hebei, only to find the head of Jiming and some remains of Gaoqing which he took to Chang'an for burial. This is basically what the requiem is about. However, the Tang Dynasty (618-907) dominated by Yang Guozhong offered such loyal martyrs nothing they deserved. It was not until Yan Zhenqing pleaded in front of Emperor Suzong (ruling from 756-762) that Honor – Conferring was made. The requiem came into being.

As described above, Yan Zhenqing, heart-broken at the thought of "Father and son perished, and their nest was destroyed", wrote the requiem with blood and tears. Being too excited and sad, Yan wrote in a rush but a natural way, producing passionate and smooth handwritings.

We can see from the original drat that the first 12 lines were an introduction to himself and praise of Jiming. He was still calm when making the narration and his handwritings were regular and forceful. But his anger and sadness peaked when he wrote "traitorous officials did not rescue", especially after "father and son perished". His writings began to follow his heart rather than rules. Font size, line spacing, and writing style varied. Mistakes and omissions increased as well. All of these made his emotional ups and downs obvious. The last two lines "If you know about this, please do not complain about being away from home for so long", especially "Alas, do partake of these offerings" were natural and vigorous.

The Chinese calligraphy art can express people's thoughts and feelings when the calligraphers have mastered the writing skills and can use the brush and ink with great flexibility. But it is complicated and difficult to master the writing skills flexibly. Yan Zhenqing was in his fifties when he wrote the requiem and had already solved the problems. In theory, he had written the well-known *Record of Twelve Questions on Calligraphy*. In calligraphy creation, he had created many renowned steles such as *Duobao Pagoda Stele* (752) and *Eulogizing a Portrait Painting of Dongfang Shuo* (753), showing that he was technically among the top calligraphers in the Tang Dynasty and even in the Chinese calligraphy history.

The so-called top-ranked calligraphy refers to those important calligraphers in the Chinese calligraphy history, such as Ouyang Xun, Yu Shinan, Chu Suiliang and Xue Ji. However, as we have mentioned, Yan Zhenqing's achievements of calligraphy, mainly *kaishu* (regular script), are higher than many important calligraphers. The *Yan* style did not reach its peak until Yan Zhenqing was in his sixties. But his *xingcao* (running-cursive script) became mature early, which was proved by the *Draft of a Requiem to My Nephew*. He formed a distinctive personal style,

Yan Zhenqing's semi-cursive script *A Letter to Liu Zhongshi*
Collected in Taipei Palace Museum

which was upright, powerful and controlled. Especially, he created a writing style called *"wu lou hen"* (writing should be like rain traces on the wall of a shabby house). But generally the influence from earlier calligraphers (mainly calligraphers in Jin and early Tang Dynasties) could still be seen in his rich and capricious writings. More than a decade later, however, his *A Letter to Liu Zhongshi* (775), which was modest and stately, marked that he had got rid of the influence of earlier calligraphers and developed a typical *Yan* style.

A Letter Beginning with "Mid-autumn" is one of the most famous calligraphic works of Wang Xianzhi (courtesy name Zijing) and is known as "the best calligraphic work by Zijing" (by Mi Fu). It is highly appreciated and remarked by calligraphers of later generations. Emperor Qianlong (1735-1799) of the Qing Dynasty (1616-1911) referred to "*Mid-autumn*" together with *A Greeting Letter Written after a Pleasant Snow* by Wang Xizhi and *A*

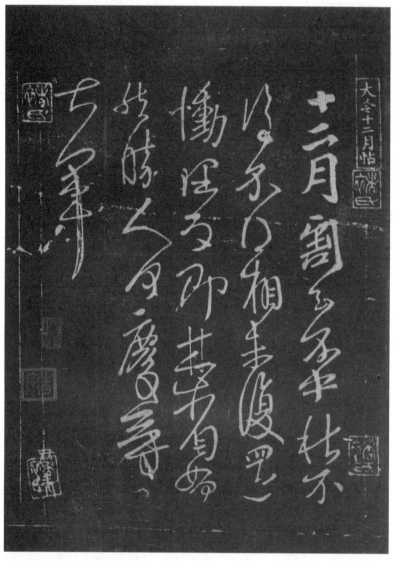

Wang Xianzhi's cursive script *Shi Er Yue Tie*

Letter to Boyuan by Wang Xun (Xizhi's nephew) as "Three Treasures" and collected them into *Three Treasures Hall Model Calligraphy*. It is now in Palace Museum in Beijing.

The *"Mid-autumn"* we see today is not the original one written by Wang Xianzhi but a copy. Some people say it was written by a calligrapher of the Tang Dynasty (618-907) while some believe that Mi Fu of the Song Dynasty (960-1279) wrote it according to *Shi Er Yue Tie* of Wang Xianzhi. *Shi Er Yue Tie* contains 32 Chinese characters and Mi Fu omitted six characters in the first sentence and four characters in the middle.

Now that it is a copy, it can more or less reflect the calligrapher's writing technique. "The thick strokes, the structure, and the writing habit are so much like those of Mi Fu" (*The Complete Works of Chinese Calligraphy* by Liu Tao, Vol. 19, page 413). Even so, the copy generally reproduced the original calligraphic work of Wang Xianzhi and demonstrated his style.

"Mid-autumn", containing 22 Chinese characters, was written in *caoshu* or *xingcao* (cursive or running-cursive script). On the right of the Chinese characters *"zhong qiu"* (Mid-autumn) were characters "Jin Wang Xianzhi zhong qiu tie" (*A Letter Beginning with "Mid-autumn"* by Wang Xianzhi), which were written by Emperor Gaozong of Song (ruling from 1162-1187). Following the text was the comment from Zhang Huaiguan: outstanding and special.

According to *Shuduan* (Judgments on Calligraphers)

by Zhang Huaiguan of the Tang Dynasty, Wang Xianzhi learned calligraphy from his father when he was young and later learned from 'sage of *caoshu*' Zhang Zhi (Boying), calligrapher of the Eastern Han Dynasty (25-220). He changed the traditional ways of writing and created his own style—"*poti*", seeking for simplicity and fluidity.

Wang Xianzhi's innovation was mainly in *caoshu* and *kaishu* (regular script). As for *caoshu*, he fully absorbed and developed the "one-stroke cursive script" of Zhang Zhi. As Zhang Huaiguan said in his *Shuduan*, "the *caoshu* of Zhang Zhi "finishes all characters in one stroke and makes them connected to each other. The possible interruption does not influence the fluidness. Only Wang Zijing knows what the writing really means. The first character will not be finished until the last one is done. The well-known 'one-stroke cursive script' starts from Zhang Zhi and is developed by Wang Xianzhi". The "one-stroke cursive script" of Zhang Zhi emphasized flowing energy. Occasional failure to share the same stroke did not affect the flowing expression. Xianzhi mainly learnt the flowing effect of one stroke from Zhang Zhi. He innovated and developed Zhang Zhi's *caoshu* mainly in seeking for simplicity and making writing easier and more fluent. He also made changes to his father's *caoshu* by taking full advantage of "one-stroke cursive script". Therefore, Wang Xianzhi's *caoshu* was different from that of both Zhang Zhi and Wang Xizhi.

The calligraphic styles of Wang Xizhi and Wang Xianzhi (known as "The Two Wangs") were quite different. Wang Xizhi's calligraphy was graceful, controlled and muscular while Wang Xianzhi's was lively, capricious and fanciful. Zhang Huaiguan said in his *Shuduan* that "Xianzhi's calligraphy is more fanciful than Xizhi's while Xizhi's calligraphy is more graceful than Xianzhi's". Huang Tingjian of the Song Dynasty once explained the calligraphic differences of "Two Wangs" with the essay difference of Zuo Qiuming and Zhuangzi: "I once compared the *caoshu* of 'Two Wangs' with essays and found that the father's style is like Zuo Qiuming's essay and the son's is like Zhuangzi's essay. There have been few unconventional calligraphers like 'Two Wangs' since the Jin Dynasty (265-420)." The essays of Zuo Qiuming and calligraphic works of Xizhi were serious while the works of Zhuangzi and Xianzhi were carefree.

We should have the following two tips in mind when we appreciate "*Mid-autumn*".

1. Shared strokes. Have a close look at the letter, and we can find that strokes of the same character tend to be interconnected and adjacent characters tend to share strokes. For example, the two characters "zhong qiu" share a stroke, so are characters "bu fu bu de" and "shen xing ru he" respectively. Overall the letter seems to be written in one stroke, making it a masterpiece of "one-stroke cursive script". Mi Fu said in *Shushi* (History of Calligraphy) that

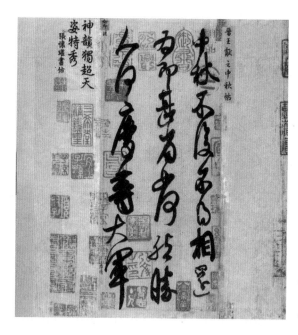

Wang Xianzhi's cursive script
Mid-autumn

"In *'Mid-autumn'*, characters are interconnected to each other as if finished in one stroke unconsciously. Therefore, it is called 'one-stroke cursive script'".

To make them more consistent and fluent, Wang Xianzhi omitted and combined some strokes, and even changed some strokes, as was shown in characters "fu" and "de". "Fu" and "de" in *kaishu* (regular script) have 12 strokes and 11 strokes separately but Xianzhi finished them in one stroke: he connected all the strokes where he shouldn't and replaced turns with curvatures.

Fluidness is very important in cursive creation, because it is the main source of cursive charm. It is fluidness that helps Wang Xianzhi to create the fanciful and lively *"Mid-*

autumn", which can make people think of the majestic momentum of rivers.

2. Application of *kaishu* in *caoshu*. Jiang Kui of the Song Dynasty wrote in his *Treatise of Calligraphy (Continued)*: "Ancient calligraphers would apply *kaishu* in their cursive writing." Sun Guoting of the Tang Dynasty wrote in *Treatise of Calligraphy*: "Zhang Zhi did not write in *kaishu* but he applied it in his cursive writing everywhere." Wang Xianzhi was the model who used *kaishu* in his cursive writing. Bao Shichen of the Qing Dynasty once wrote: "People know that regular writing is perfect in curvatures but do not know that cursive writing is ideal for dot application. This is why cursive writing is not popular. The cursive writing of Xianzhi was often finished in one stroke with no obvious start and ending. But by careful observation you will find the curvatures are full of turns." Wang Xianzhi applied dots of *kaishu* in cursive writing and would "change forces at each move" in curvatures.

Taking the character "deng" in *"Mid-autumn"* as example, Wang Xianzhi combined the last two strokes (vertical hook and dot) in one and added turns in the curvature. Looking closely and you will find that the curvature is not round but composed of several short moves. This is the effect of *kaishu* in cursive writing.

Stele Inscription in the Confucius Temple by Yu Shinan

Tang Wenyuan

Yu Shinan was a very famous master of calligraphy in the early Tang Dynasty (618-907).

Yu Shinan (558-638), style name (*zi*) Boshi, was born in Yuezhou (today's Yuyao in Zhejiang). He was a paramount official and Lord of Yongxing County so he was also called Yu Yongxing. He died in the 12th year of Zhenguan Period of the Tang dynasty (638) when he was 81 and was conferred the Minister of Rites and the posthumous title Duke Wenyi.

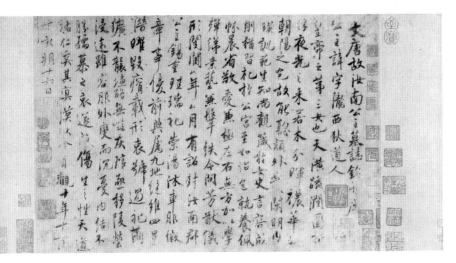

Yu Shinan's *Stele Inscription in the Epitaph of Princess Ru'nan*
Collected in Shanghai Museum

Shinan was a quiet man with few desires who was determined, diligent and good at writing. During the reign of Emperor Taizong (ruling from 626 to 649), he was military staff officer of the official residence of Qin and Academician in charge of official documents and correspondence with Fang Xuanling. Yu Shinan had a remarkable memory. Once Emperor Taizong of the Tang Dynasty asked him to write *The Biographies of Exemplary Women* on the screen to enjoy but could not find the book immediately. Yu Shinan then wrote down the whole book from his memory, which was highly praised by Emperor Taizong. Emperor Taizong appreciated Shinan's talents and often talked with him about classics and history. Each time they came to the political gains and losses of former

105

emperors, Shinan would offer advice and warnings to the emperor. Emperor Taizong once praised him and said, "Yu Shinan was a man of five absolute merits (including virtue, loyalty, knowledge, diction and letters)." He also said, "A minister can be good enough with one of the five merits but Shinan owns all."

Some famous calligraphers in the early Tang dynasty wrote in *kaishu* (regular script), especially *xiaokai* (small regular script). Although they followed the style of Jin dynasty (265-420), their works were not as free and unrestricted as those in the Wei (220-265) and Jin dynasties. Only Yu Shinan took the essence and became more skillful after learning from the monk Zhiyong in the Sui Dynasty (581-618). Just as *Xuanhe Calligraphic Florilegium* put, "Monk Zhiyong is very good at calligraphy and has got the essence of Wang Xizhi so Shinan goes to learn from him. Shinan works hard and pays off. His writing in *kaishu* in his old age can even compare with that of Wang Xizhi". With his artistic accomplishment and intelligence, and steady and elegant handwriting, we can say that his calligraphy is better than his teacher Zhiyong.

Yu Shinan was in his old age and also his most prestigious period in the early Tang Dynasty. At that time, Emperor Taizong of the Tang Dynasty was very fond of Wang Xizhi's calligraphy and Yu Shinan managed to fully express the merits of the writing styles of Wang Xizhi and

Wang Xianzhi. He wrote *Stele Inscription in the Confucius Temple* and *the Epitaph of Princess Ru'nan* (the original writing) and many others in this period. Unfortunately, the works did not survive. Only some copies remained. Since the Song dynasty (960-1279) till now, only the *Stele Inscription in the Confucius Temple* among all Yu Shinan's works has passed down from generation to generation. *Du Mu* recorded that, "I once saw Shinan's calligraphic work called *Stele Inscription in the Confucius Temple* which was offered to Taizong. Taizong gave Shinan the huangyinyin (seal made of silver and bronze) of Wang Xizhi in return, showing how precious his calligraphic work could be".

The most famous and most popular calligraphic work of Yu Shinan is the *Stele Inscription in the Confucius Temple*. The stele inscription mainly recorded that on December 29th of the ninth year of Wude during the reign of Emperor Gaozu of the Tang Dynasty (ruling from 618-626), Kong Delun, the 23rd generation male descendant of Confucius, was conferred marquisate and that the Confucius Temple was renovated. Chancellor Yang Shidao and others suggested that a stele should be erected. So Yu Shinan was asked to write an essay on the stele in red ink, namely *Stele Inscription in the Confucius Temple*. The stele did not have a title until the third year of Chang'an, when the minister Wang Dan added *Stele of Confucius Temple in the Zhou Dynasty* above the inscription and the detailed time below. In November of the fifth year of Dazhong during the reign of Emperor Xuanzong of the Tang Dynasty, Prime Minister Feng Shen suggested that "Zhou Dynasty" should be replaced by "Tang Dynasty". The stele is as high as four meters and as wide as one meter and a half. It was finished in the seventh year of Zhenguan during the reign of Emperor Taizong of the Tang Dynasty. There were more than 3,000 Chinese characters into 40 lines with 84 characters in each line. The majestic stele was written by Yu Shinan when he was 69. So it was a masterpiece in Yu Shinan's old ages. The calligraphic art of the stele achieved a high accomplishment. The strokes were nice and plump, tender yet forceful. The structure and font style were slim and elegant. Have a careful look at the rubbings from the Tang Dynasty collected by Li Zonghan (now in Japan), and you can easily find that all the characters of the inscription were written with standard strokes and in a flowing style, making people feel peaceful and upright. All strokes were written subtly and made up flowing veins: vigorous, harmonious, and forceful. The special way of Yu Shinan to write the Chinese character "ge" was particularly exquisite. Even Emperor Taizong of the Tang Dynasty learned and imitated it. All in all, Yu Shinan greatly influenced later calligraphers, including Ouyang Xun and Chu Suiliang (two of the "Four Masters of the Early Tang Dynasty"). Xie Jin once wrote that "Yu Shinan taught Ouyang Xun and Chu Suiliang; Chu Suiliang taught Xue Ji. This is how the 'Four

One of Yu Shinan's *Stele Inscription in the Confucius Temple* Collected in Japanese Mitsui Memorial Museum

Masters of the Early Tang Dynasty' came into being."
Chu Suiliang, in particular, learned his earliest and most
basic strokes from Yu Shinan and therefore found the way
to learn from Wang Xizhi. Calligraphers after the Tang
Dynasty, famous or not, all made great efforts to learn Yu
Shinan's calligraphy style. Yu Shinan contributed a lot to
calligraphy by serving as a link between past and future.
His calligraphy was also very influential in Dongying
(Today's Japan), where calligraphers of many dynasties
also absorbed nutrition from his works. In addition, he was
also an excellent calligraphy theorist whose theories were
acknowledged by many scholars.

The *Stele Inscription in the Confucius Temple* written
by Yu Shinan was serious yet free and tender yet forceful,
becoming a model for later generations. Liu Xizai in the
Qing Dynasty (1616-1911) once said that learning from
Yu Shinan's calligraphy should focus on the essence of his
writing style, which was fully exhibited through the *Stele
Inscription in the Confucius Temple*. The *Stele Inscription
in the Confucius Temple* was burnt not long after it was
finished. The rubbings of the original stele were rare even
in the Northern Song Dynasty (960-1127). Huang Tingjian
once wrote a poem to express how valuable the stele could
be. Now two copies are commonly seen, one is in the Forest
of Stone Tablets of Xi'an, Shaanxi Province and one is
in Chengwu County, Shandong Province. The former one
was inscribed by Wang Yanchao in the early Song Dynasty

and was called Shaan version, or West Temple or plump version because of the plump writing style. The latter one was inscribed in the Yuan Dynasty (1206-1368) and was called Chengwu version, or East Temple or slim version because of the slim writing style. Shaan version is more famous while Chengwu version is better in font style and writing skills. As Weng Fanggang once said, Shaan version was better in plump expression but Chengwu version was better in expressing Yu Shinan's writing intentions. The Chengwu version, with primitive simplicity and crude beauty, is almost nothing different from the original one.

Liu Gongquan and Calligraphy

Liu Gongquan, a calligrapher, was recorded in history for regular script.

Liu Gongquan (778-865), was a calligrapher living in the mid-Tang Dynasty (766-835). He was born in Huayuan (today's Yaoxian county, Shaanxi province). He devoted his life to Confucian-classic study, especially in the *Book of Songs,* the *Book of History (Shu), Spring and Autumn Annals (Zuoshi Chunqiu), Guoyu* and *Zhuangzi,*

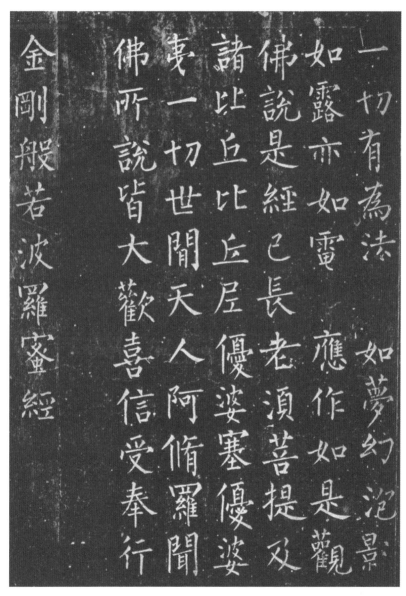

金剛般若波羅蜜經

佛所說皆大歡喜信受奉行‥‥

東一切世間天人阿脩羅聞

諸比丘比丘尼優婆塞優婆

佛說是經已長老須菩提及

如露亦如電應作如是觀

一切有為法如夢幻泡景

Part of the *Diamond Sutra* (*Vajracchedika-sutra*) by Liu Gongquan in his early times

113

and knew a a certain of tonality. In the beginning of his political career, his calligraphic works impeded him. Emperor Muzong (795-824) was fond of Liu's calligraphic works and gave him a low position Shu Xueshi. While Liu devoted a lot to this job for three dynasties. He was an honest and loyal person. It was said that, when Emperor Muzong asked him how to hold the bush straight, he answered that holding a straight characteristics in priority. Later generations called this as"Bi Jian", to remonstrate by calligraphy-teaching.

His brother Liu Qizhi then served in the army. Liu Qizhi wrote a letter to the prime minister to help his brother get the promotion. That was the first promotion for Liu Gongquan. Not until the first year of Xiantong period (860-874), did he got the second promotion. Finally, he died at the age of eighty-eight.

Due to the appreciation of emperors, his calligraphic works were precious. Emperor Wenzong (809-840) once praised his work better than Zhong Xi's and Wang Xizhi's. He even carved Liu Gongquan's works of regular script, cursive script and running script on coins. Thus Liu's reputation wildly spread that people were eager to get his calligraphy works. Some foreign officials even bought Liu's works by the government funds.

Liu also had a good reputation in poem-composing. His poem even saved a concubine's life from the Emperor .

Liu Gongquan was famous at his time, and in one

thousand years later too. His stele inscriptions are still renowned, *The Mysterious Pagoda Stele Inscription* is the most famous. It was finished in the form of regular script in 841, on which some of the characters were faded. But that cannot prevent it from popularity. The original stele is reserved in the Forest of Stone Tablets of Xi'an.

His another masterpiece in regular script was Shencenjun Stele, or a Tablet Recording Emperor's Inspection of the Imperial (wrote by Cui Xuan) which was finished in 843 when Liu Gongquan was 66. Since it was built in the imperial palace that people barely had the access to copy it, this tablet was not famous. It was divided into two volumes, and the first one was kept at Beijing Library. Besides the Cultural Relics Press issued with the photocopy version. However the second volume was lost long before.

Liu Gongquan also has many other regular scripts like the Diamond Sutra(Vajracchedika-sutra). While some of the original versions were lost and some are faded too much to read. So they were not famous as the previous twos.

His running script did not spread much. So Lanting Poem was the most famous. Dong Qichang once edited it into *Xihong Tang Tie*. The Emperor Qianlong (1711-1799) was fond of it and re-edited it into the fifth volume of *Lanting Bazhu Tie*. Thus it is accessible for us. Meng Zhao Tie also called as Hanlin Tie was another his famous

Liu Gongquan's *Shencejun Stele*

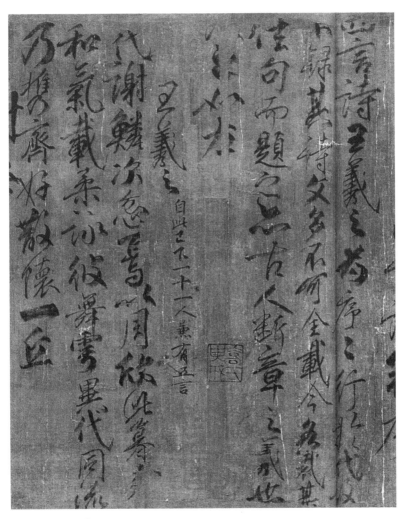

Parts of Liu Gongquan's Mysterious Pagoda Stele Inscription and *Orchid Pavilion Poems*, reserved in the Palace Museum, Beijing,China

running script. Meng Zhao Tie was finished at the age of 44 in 821. His style in calligraphy was believed to represent the uniqueness at his time.

Liu started his calligraphy study from Wang Xizhi, then learnt from many other calligraphers in Sui Dynasty (581-618) and Tang Dynasty (618-907). He created his own style based on previous calligraphy works. Fan Zhongyan from Song Dynasty (960-1279) praised Liu's style and Yan Zhenqing's style and called them as Yanjin Liugu.

While comments on Liu's style from later generations varied. In general, there were more people out there speaking highly of his style. Someone believed his style had illustrated perfectness. However, someone thought his style was not good as Yan Zhenqing's. When it came to the mid-to-end of the Qing Dynasty (1776-1911), some people thought his style useless.

To some extent, Liu's style may be a little bit deliberate and dull. While we cannot ignore how brilliant his style was. You may take in Liu's style through his calligraphy works.

A Brief Talk about the "Crazy" Zhang and "Drunk" Su

The Tang Dynasty is the peak in the history of Chinese calligraphy, and one of the signs is that a large number of calligraphers emerged. Many famous calligraphers, such as Ouyang Xun, Yu Shinan, Chu Suiliang, Li Yong, Sun Guoting, Yan Zhenqin and Liu Gongquan, all belonged to that period. But talking about the most romantic ones, they must be Zhang Xu and Huai Su, the two greatest *caoshu*(cursive) calligraphers.

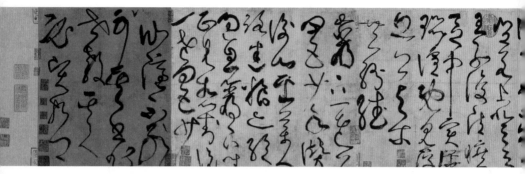

Four Poems written by Zhang Xu

Zhang Xu was a chancellor in county, while Huaisu was a monk at that time. The two seems irrelevant to each other, but why we think them romantic and even put them together to talk about? They surely have something in common. It is said in *Shulin Chronicle that*:

Zhang Xu was fond of bottle. Every time he got drunk to chant loudly and stride crazily, he began to write; or he dipped his head in ink and then wrote with the head. When he "got awake", he saw the writing and got surprised for it was too perfect to be imitated. As for Huaisu, he was a bold and unconstrained person not sticking to trifles. Huaisu was also fond of bottle and would get drunk several times a day, so his work was called "Drunken Monk's Writing". Every time he got drunk in high spirits, he would write on walls, clothes or wares. He once talked about his drunk writing, "The works he wrote when drunk cannot be duplicated when awake."

We can get several conclusions from the above two records. First, Zhang Xu was fond of bottle and got drunk,

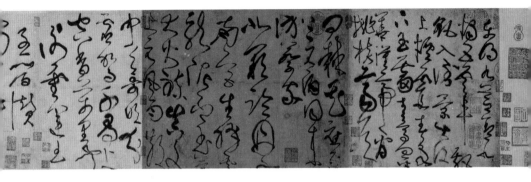

and so did Huaisu. From "Be getting drunk nine times a day", we know the two calligraphers were both tipplers, maybe also with "great capacity for liquor". Second, they often wrote while getting drunk, which often brought out dramatic effects. For example, Zhang Xu often "chanted loudly and strode crazily" or "dipped his head in ink"; while Huaisu often "got drunk in high spirits and would write on walls, clothes or wares". Their creating scenes are totally different from those of other calligraphers. Third, they were both proud of their works created when drunk. Zhang Xu was "surprised at his writing, thinking it too perfect to be imitated"; Huaisu also said "The works he wrote when drunk cannot be duplicated after awake".

Zhang Xu and Huaisu did have an affinity with liquor. Zhuangzi had said, "make him drunk to watch his attitude" (*Liezi* of *Zhuangzi*). Perhaps when intoxicated, calligraphers can express their creative thoughts and emotions thoroughly. Of course, there should be also a fourth reason: Zhang Xu and Huaisu shared a reputation of *caosheng* ("sage of cursive script" in Chinese). They were good at *kuangcao* ("mad cursive script"), which is one of the most free-spirited and least restraint style of *caoshu*("cursive script"), and obviously very attractive to uninhibited Zhang Xu and Huaisu. They were both extraordinarily good at drinking and *caoshu*, but these can't qualify them as a master or *caosheng*. In learning, had they also some distinctive characteristics? It was recorded in *Catalogue of Calligraphies Compiled during the Xuanhe Reign Period* that:

(Zhang Xu) got his calligraphic style from seeing heavers fighting for the roads, understood the calligraphic meaning when hearing someone playing the instrument and learned its essence when watching Mrs. Gongsun brandishing a sword.

Zhu Changwen's *Sequel to the Judgment on Calligraphy* also recorded:

(Huaisu) got enlightened when watching summer cloud changing with the wind, which seemed like a warrior drawing a sword, vivid and moving.

Zhang Xu and Huaisu were not those who were conservative and unable to adapt. They were not only engrossed in learning the ancients' rules, but also paid more attention to learn from the nature. He tried to understand the art of calligraphy through persistent pursuit, mature thinking and meticulous observation, thus to get inspiration and enlightenment on learning. This learning method is commendable in ancient calligraphers of each dynasty.

They also held a huge enthusiasm for their own artistic careers, with great care, exploring each opportunity to comprehend. At the same time, they observed the natural world not just staying on the surface, but taking efforts to explore the inner essence and value of things below the surface, making it a starting point for comprehending. Most people may forget such occasions soon like two carriers fighting their ways and summer cloud changing. But they were good at finding a certain "meaning"manifested in these natural phenomena and obtaining a more profound revelation from them. Thus, the artistic images they created naturally featured more vitality. Their successor calligraphers in the Song Dynasty, like Su Dongpo, Huang Shangu and Wen Yuke, had also inherited this excellent learning method: Huang Shangu learned his technique of writing when seeing boaters rowing; Wen Yuke got a great progress in his *caoshu* after seeing a taoist priest fighting with a snake. These are all excellent illusions of getting "Enlightenment" from the nature.

In addition to not being engrossed in learning the ancients' rules, Zhang Xu and Huaisu are all very hardworking in study. Zhu Changwen said in his *Sequel to the Judgements on Calligraphy*:

(Zhang Xu) was so obsessed with calligraphy that it could not be changed by power and money; he was satisfied to devote all his life and energy to calligraphy... At the beginning, when he was the governor of Changshu, an old man went to sue, but the old man came back again a few days after being sentenced. Zhang Xu got angry and blamed: "Why do you repeatedly disturb the government with trifles!" The old man said: "You have a wonderful handwriting, so I am trying to get and hide it in my small case. In fact, I have nothing to sue." Therefore the old man was requested to take out all his possession of handwriting. Zhang Xu was surprised, "They were all masterpieces." Since then, he got a great progress in his technique of writing.

This is a very interesting story. Zhang Xu's handwriting was very marvelous, but he still showed a great interest in the old man's collection and thus got a great benefit, showing his great interest in calligraphy. No wonder Zhu Changwen praised, "With great intelligence, you still learn from others and will never stop learning."

Besides the records, there were also real objects which can prove Zhang Xu's diligence. His *Stone Pillar to the Inscriptions about Court Gentlemen* is entirely the extremely-neat *zhengkai* (real regular script) with tight rules. Dong You said it "vague and rigid with a tight venation" and Wang Yanshan even believed he could match Ouyang Xun, Yu Shinan and other masters of *kaishu*, so we can see his great achievements in *kaishu*.

Huaisu is even more hardworking. According to the

Zhang Xu's *The Stomachache Note(Du Tong Tie)*

third volume of Ma Zonghuo's *Shulin Chronicle*:

He was so diligent that his used pens were buried and heaped up to form a pen mound. When living in Lingling, he was so poor that he could not afford to write on paper, so he planted tens of thousands palms to write on the leaves, thus his house was named "green sky". Short of paper, he would find a plate to write on, or to write on a board repeatedly, and finally the plate and board were all worn out.

Zhang Xu and Huaisu achieved their fame with their unconditional love in calligraphy and a kind of hard and strenuous spirit. It was well said, "Don't decentralize your mind on what you are doing." It is difficult to understand its real value if we only see their romantic manner, so you

125

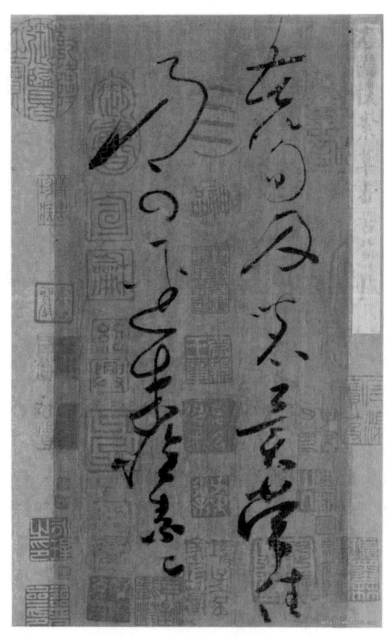

Photography of Collation of Lyrics by Zhang Xiaoxiang

should pay attention to what they spent on exploration.

Unrestrained enthusiasm, flexible learning methods, preference for *caoshu*, coupled with interesting records about their fondness on liquor, together shaped the two romantic images of Zhang Xu and Huaisu–a historical calligrapher image. People often like to call them "crazy Zhang and drunk Su". According to Zhu Changwen's *Sequel to the Judgements on Calligraphy*, the later calligrapher master Yan Zhenqing, also humorously expressed his opinion:

Before, official Zhang was called "crazy Zhang" for his calligraphic works, now can I call Huaisu "mad monk" to continue the "crazy Zhang"?

Zhang Xu and Huaisu hold an extremely important position in the history of Chinese calligraphy. First, they broke the situation of *kaishu's* domination and enriched the forms of calligraphy in the Tang Dynasty through their bold breakthrough in *caoshu*. Second, they reached an unprecedented height in *caoshu* through effective artistic practice and relentless innovations. Before the Tang Dynasty, there were few achievements in *caoshu*, so Zhang Xu's and Huaisu's *caoshu* refreshed people for its structure, strokes and other aspects. Its structure, strokes, lines and even its momentum and verve all made people stunning. Later Huang Tingjian and Zhu Yunming got much art nutrition from him; and Yan Zhenqing even consulted to them directly. The content of their discussions were recorded in the two passage of *Yan Zhenqing's Explanation* on *Meaning of Zhang Xu's twelve strokes* and *Discussion on Caoshu Between Huaisu and Yan Zhenqing*. It can be said Yan Zhenqing's later achievements were inseparable from Zhang Xu and Huaisu's instruction.

Again, Zhang Xu and Huaisu' *caoshu* was not only a pioneering work for the previous generation, but also affected a large number of calligraphers in the future generation; at the same time, their academy purpose of calligraphy had also played an important role during the formation of the future calligraphic style. The charm and affection they showed in *kuangcao*, their unconventional calligraphic styles and personalities greatly inspired the formation of the trend of self-expression in the Song Dynasty. In other words, the two *caoshu* calligraphers of the Tang Dynasty also virtually became a guide for *self-expression* calligraphic style in the Song Dynasty.

Xuanhe Calligraphic Florilegium, written in the Song Dynasty, included Zhang Xu's twenty-four calligraphic works and one hundred and one of Huaisu's, really a large number, all imperial and secret troves, besides the *Stone Pillar to the Inscriptions about Court Gentlemen*. Unfortunately, as dynasties passed, many were lost and few were left. In recent years, Zhang Xu's *Four Poems*, and Huaisu's *Autobiography*, *On Calligraphy*, *Fish-eating* and *Bitter Bamboo Shoots* have been published, arousing a great interest of many calligraphy lovers. Perhaps they can visualize the status of "crazy" Zhang and "drunk" Su.

Mengying, an eminent monk of the Northern Song Dynasty (960-1127), got well-known by people because of his several inscriptions on tablets. They are: *The Content of Source of the Side of Character* in seal script, *The Thousand Character Classic* in seal script and *Notes to the Confucian Temple* in regular script. Mengying lived in the early period of the Northern Song Dynasty. The Northern Song Dynasty was founded for a short

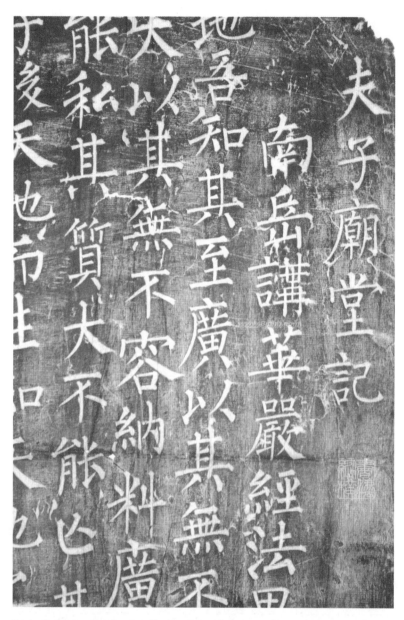

Part of *Notes to the Confucian Temple* in regular script of Mengying

time after the Five Dynasties and Ten Kingdoms (907-960). Literary works during that time were vulgar, so were the art of calligraphy and painting. In order to make official standard of character, the imperial officials assigned Xu Xuan, a literary scholar and calligrapher of the Northern Song Dynasty, to proofread *The Analytical Dictionary of Chinese Characters*. Meanwhile, the government encouraged the study of characters and got a wide collection of excellent calligraphy works of former dynasties. Lots of literary people tried every effort to make their works popular. Gou Zhongzheng, a scholar of the Northern Song Dynasty, handed in his calligraphy work, *The Classic of Filial Piety*, which he wrote in three styles of calligraphy. Li Jianzhong, a calligrapher at that time, also donated his works to the government. He imitated the style of handwriting of former calligraphers and finished *The Classic of Filial Piety*. Under circumstance like this, Mengying delved into the study of characters and finished *The Content of Source of the Side of Character* in seal script, meanwhile, he proved that there were eighteen different styles of seal script and he imitated these styles of seal script. And Mengying got famous for his "jade chopstick style" inscription, another form of seal script. After that, he went to Bianliang (Today's Kaifeng of Henan Province), the capital city of the Northern Song Dynasty and was summoned by Zhao Guangyi, emperor Taizong of the Song Dynasty. Mengying was awarded a purple robe which signified certain official ranking by the emperor. After this, Mengying's name got widely spread and he got well-known.

Though Mengying got popularity, people did not know much about his life. All the records of his life were simple and short. In Zhu Changwen's book (Zhu Changwen, a famous calligraphy theorist of the Northern Song Dynasty), the record of Mengying's life was complete. "Mengying was from the Northern Song Dynasty, his hometown was Quzhou in Zhejiang Province. He proved that there were eighteen different styles of seal script and imitated them while he did well in the'jade chopstick style' inscription. Once he went to the capital city of the Northern Song Dynasty, he was summoned to meet Emperor Taizong of Song and was awarded a purple robe by the emperor. When he was old, he travelled in the southern area and died there. Many distinguished literary scholars wrote poems to praise and memorize Mengying. Xuanyi was Mengying's Buddhist given name which was a symbol of his excellence. Besides Mengying, there were also other monks who were good at imitating the handwriting of former distinguished calligraphers. For example, Haobin imitated Wang Xizhi's handwriting, Mengzheng imitated Liu Gongquan's calligraphy and Wanji was good at the imitation of Yan Zhenqing's handwriting. These monks who were good at calligraphy got popular and people praised their excellence of handwriting."

The stele of *Rebuilding of Queen Mother's Palace*

Reviewing the whole life of Mengying, he was awarded a purple robe by the emperor and lots of famous scholars wrote poems for him when he was old. These two things made Mengying's life splendid. As a monk, Mengying was the only one who got so popular and well-known because of his excellent calligraphy. In the first year of Xianping (998), a stele called *Poems for Mengying* was erected in Xi'an. A monk called Zhengmeng inscribed on the stele. The inscription was a collection of poems that were written by scholars at that time for Mengying. It can be seen from this that nearly all the scholars wrote poems for Mengying to compliment him. And nearly all of these poets were a little complimentary. There were about more than thirty scholars who wrote poems and expressed their approvals for Mengying. How popular Mengying was at that time!

Reading these poems about Mengying, the life of Mengying can be better understood. Mengying was just nineteen years old when he was summoned and awarded a purple robe by the emperor. Obviously, Mengying enjoyed success when he was young. Mengying received high reputation and got popular at that time for nearly forty years after that. And he made these achievements during the early time of the Northern Song Dynasty. During that time, Mengying completed most of his inscriptions on tablets. Mengying's famous inscriptions on tablets were as followings: *The Thousand Character Classic* in seal script,

Eighteen Styles of Seal Script, *Notes to the Confucian Temple* in regular script, *Rebuilding of Queen Mother's Palace* in running script which was written by Tao Gu, a governor of the Northern Song Dynasty and *The Preface of The Biography of Eminent Monks in the Northern Song Dynasty* whose author was also Tao Gu.

The Content of Source of the Side of Character in seal script was another calligraphy work of Mengying. Mengying was so talented that he mastered skills of several styles of calligraphy, such as seal script, clerical script, regular script, running script and cursive script. However, his seal script was the most famous at that time. Li Yangbing, a distinguished calligrapher of the Tang Dynasty (618-907), was very good at seal script. Li's calligraphic works of seal script have profound influence at the beginning of the Northern Song Dynasty. Mengying was proud of his seal script and a little self-conceited boosting himself the best successor of Li Yangbing's seal script. People at that time also believed that. *The Content of Source of the Side of Character* in seal script was one of the Mengying's satisfied works. At the end of it, there were author's preface and a replied letter of Guo Zhongshu, a famous painter of the Northern Song Dynasty. In Mengying's preface at the end of the book, Mengying praised Li Yangbing a lot and depreciated other calligraphers of seal script such as Li Si, a great statesman of Qin Dynasty (221BC-207BC). We should admit the fact that Mengying strove to imitate Li Yangbing's handwriting and got the essence of Li's calligraphy. However, Li Yangbing's calligraphy had weaknesses, too. So people criticized Li Yangbing and Mengying. Since clerical script and cursive script got popular, people learned about seal script according to *The Analytical Dictionary of Chinese characters* which attaches great importance to *xiaozhuan* (later seal script developed in the Qin Dynasty). *Dazhuan* (ancient seal script developed in the late Xizhou Dynasty (1046BC-771BC)) did not get people's attention. The seal script Li Yangbing and Mengying learned was just a small part of the original one. They lost some features of the original seal script. With the of society, the art of calligraphy also changed a lot.

Guo Zhongshu, a painter of the Northern Song Dynasty, he made research about Li Yangbing and his calligraphy, too. However, Guo had a much clearer understanding than Mengying. At the end of *The Content of Source of the Side of Character*, there was Guo's replied letter to Mengying. Guo pointed out there were some mistakes about the analysis of the side of characters because Mengying referred to a book wrote by Lin Han, a scholar at that time. In Guo's opinion, Lin Han's book would mislead people. In this letter, it can be seen clearly that Guo Zhongshu satirized Mengying in some way. However, Mengying's work had profound meanings in terms of remaining some ancient literary works.

Apart from seal script, Mengying's regular script deserved compliments. He imitated Liu Gongquan's style of calligraphy when he created *Notes to the Confucian Temple*. Liu Gongquan was a famous calligrapher of the Tang Dynasty who was famous for regular script. While Mengying's regular script was not as good as Liu's. As for *The Content of Source of the Side of Character*, Mengying imitated Ouyang Xun's style of calligraphy to write preface at the end. Besides, as the sentence in one poem which was used to praise Mengying, Mengying not only learned regular script from Ouyang Xun but also learned running script from Yu Shinan. Apart from seal script and regular script, Mengying was also good at running script. *The Rebuilding of Queen Mother's Palace* was his calligraphy work in running script.

The Rebuilding of Queen Mother's Palace was written by Tao Gu, a governor at that time. Tao Gu once wrote a book called *The Notebook of Trifles*. Mengying worked together with Tao Gu for several times. Mengying once transcribed Tao Gu's book, *The Biography of Eminent Monks*. And Tao Gu's wrote preface for Mengying's *The Thousand Character Classic* in seal script. In his preface, Tao Gu praised Mengying's seal script. Tao Gu thought highly of Mengying. Tao Gu once transcribed his own work, *The Rebuilding of Queen Mother's Palace*, however, officials at that time were not satisfied with Tao Gu's transcription and asked Mengying to transcribe it.

There were some mistakes in Mengying's transcription so Mengying confronted with questions. With the development of society, more and more people became to criticize Mengying's calligraphy works. Some scholars expressed their opinions about Mengying. One of them pointed out that the transcription of Mengying contrasted the original work of Tao Gu.

The most severe disagreement on Mengying was about his proving of eighteen styles of seal script and his imitation of the eighteen styles of seal script. *Xuanhe Calligraphic Florilegium*, a collection of calligraphic works, did not have records of Mengying's conclusion about eighteen styles of seal script. For a long time, there were lots of calligraphers who were able to write in different styles of calligraphy. However, people believed that those calligraphers only wanted to gain popularity and show off their skills. Following Mengying, some calligraphers learnt from fifty-six styles of calligraphy or even more. The authority at that time thought highly of Mengying's proving of eighteen styles of seal script. And lots of people follow the example of Mengying. However, Mengying made such conclusion according to his thoughts rather than depending on the evidence. Much more evidence was found to prove Mengying's conclusion about eighteen styles of seal script was wrong.

Mengying also had his own literary works on calligraphic theory, such as *On Eighteen Styles of Seal*

Script. Apart from that, he made conclusions in some of his articles and literary works, while these conclusions did not have enough evidence to prove their authenticity. Mengying was fond of seal script while his handwriting did not abide by the rules and regulations. This was his weakness. Meanwhile, Mengying was able to write poems and articles. However, Mengying's poems failed to be handed down from the past generations. Obviously, Mengying was able to write poems but he did not specialize in it.

The Jin and Tang dynasties are two peak periods in the history of Chinese calligraphy when countless brilliant classical calligraphic works and prominent calligraphers were born. Wang Xizhi's Wei and Jin-based calligraphic style of gentleness and elegance has led calligraphy world for a long time. Generations of calligraphers have admired and learned his calligraphic style. Nevertheless, when the young and ambitious Huang Tingjian just

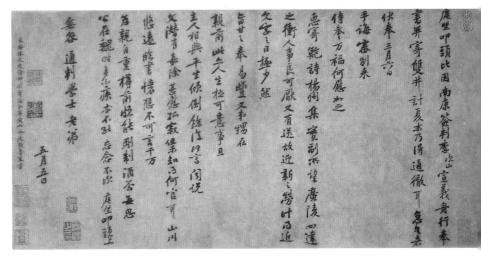

Huang Tingjian's cursive writing of *Nankang Tie*, Collected in Taipei Palace Museum

entered the calligraphy circle, what he saw was messy calligraphy styles in the Song Dynasty. Calligraphers of traditionalism represented by Li Jianzhong and Cai Xiang advocated to inherit the calligraphic styles of the Jin and Tang dynasties and pleased themselves with abiding by traditional style; Calligraphers of innovation represented by Su Dongpo called for embodiment of temperament and expression of their feelings in their calligraphic works, working to break a new ground in calligraphy. In the Song Dynasty, confrontation between traditional and innovative groups was not severe and the calligraphic style of appreciating implications that became the mainstream later was not mature. Under such circumstance, Huang Tingjian realized that he could accomplish much in this field.

Huang Tingjian chose to stand on the side of Su Dongpo without hesitation partly because he was Su' student or because he had something in common with Su in calligraphy. He played a major role in the group of appreciating implications and left many precious calligraphy legacy for later generations. Meanwhile, he was of high attainment in religious study, which made his calligraphic style seem unique even in the group of appreciating implications. His style evolved into an independent stream out of Su Dongpo and other excellent calligraphers. We say Su's calligraphy obviously reflects Laozi and Zhuangzi's philosophy of governing by non-interference and being indifferent to fame and wealth. Similarly, Huang' calligraphy shows Buddhism spirit of purity and calm. Although Huang and Su both adhered to the same principle of appreciating implications, the differences between their styles are still evident.

Huang's calligraphic style was extremely unique. He replaced restraint with wildness, represented completeness with looseness, showed flatness with inclination and combined bluntness with sharpness, which was greatly different from the regular script in the Jin and Tang dynasties.

His calligraphic structure was inclined to tilt but stayed balance with sharp cuttings and elasticity. Those elegant Jin people and honest Tang people did not condescend nor dare to put themselves in such a high-spirited style. In a certain sense, he deviated from *Kaishu*, even farther than Su Dongpo. In other words, he maintained few *Kaishu* rules in his calligraphy.

Huang Tingjian, who once claimed to be an ill monk in temple, made great accomplishments in Zen Buddhism. In calligraphy, I can also taste his Bodhidharma-like persistency. Da Chongguang from the Qing Dynasty once said:

This is the beauty of tasting Huang's calligraphic style. What's the impression left by Huang Tingjian? "A holy leisure monk". Monks are always thin due to vegetarian diets. A leisure monk has a sense of unrestrained tolerance.

Therefore, we can know the basic features of Huang's calligraphy: 1. Slim: sharp strokes and bony composition; 2. Varied: unconstrained structure and free style, consistent with the concise and to-the-point comment of Da Chongguang. Of course, the most important is that Da Chongguang believed that the calligraphic style of Huang came from his "proficiency in the Zen". The calligraphic works of Chu Suiliang, Yan Zhenqing, and Zhao Mengfu did not have religious expression. A broad Buddhism rather than the Zen cannot reveal the essence of Huang's calligraphy even though there is religious atmosphere; the "monk" alone is too limited; only the monk is free-minded enough can the appearance of a dignitary be obvious: a monk after painstaking cultivation becomes enlightened

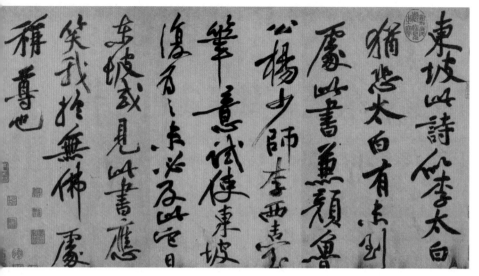

Huang Tingjian's cursive writing *Postcript of Su Shi's Han Shi Tie*, collected in Taipei Palace Museum

suddenly and even can criticize the Buddhistic tenets. It is the same with Huang's calligraphy, whether in writing skill or basic style.

Compared with the *caoshu* (cursive script) of Huang Tingjian, his *xingshu* (semi-cursive script) applied more side strokes. The characters were compact inside while broad outside so that they were called "radiations" with obvious turns and strong rhythms. His *caoshu* was full of changes, greatly demonstrating his literary talents. But no matter how much the structure changed, the bony and slant feature remained. He never used thick ink or plump or serious strokes. Instead, he always exhibited his exquisite skills and rich emotional expressions through slim yet forceful strokes, occupation of blank space, and changes of writing speed. Even the plump writing of Su Dongpo or compact writing of Mi Yuanzhang could not compare. The Zen expression in Huang's calligraphic works was not only distinctive in thoughts but also in appearance; so he stood out among the numerous masters with his unique calligraphic outlooks, stroke expression, space occupation, and the special Zen in particular.

During the long history of Chinese calligraphy, there have been a lot of calligraphic masters who converted to Buddhism. Monk Zhiyong in the Six Dynasties (222-589) was believed to be a descendant of Wang Xizhi and his *kaishu* (regular script) was following the style of Wang indeed; Monk Huaisu in the Tang Dynasty (618-907) was a great master of *caoshu* and art; Monks Foyin, Canliao, Yan Fahua, and Dignitary Nan were all known to be proficient in calligraphy and there were even more such people in the Ming and Qing dynasties (1368-1911). But comparing their works with the "Zen calligraphy" of Huang Tingjian, we can find that the religious calligraphers produced worldly works as monks with little religious expression. Huang studied Zen without converting to Buddhism but his calligraphic works were full of Zen atmosphere, an example of worldly people producing Buddhist works. The corresponding phenomenon was quite thought-provoking. Therefore, whether the calligraphic works convey religious expressions or not depends not on the identities of the calligraphers but on the artistic spirit of the works.

The combination of calligraphy and Zen had a close relationship with the once popular meditation practice among scholar officials in the Song Dynasty (960-1279). Before the Song Dynasty, Zen was not popular and the scholars had not been closely linked with religion, so the calligraphers at that time lacked objective conditions to produce "Zen calligraphy". After the Yuan Dynasty (1206-1368), the popularity and promotion of Zen weakened its own characteristics, making it not as pure as the Zen in the Song Dynasty and nothing different from the culture and art. By comparison, the Song Dynasty was the most ideal age. Su Dongpo and Mi Yuanzhang among the Four Great Masters of the Song Dynasty both tried to add Zen elements into their calligraphy. but limited by their artistic conditions, they did not get a full success. It was at that time that Huang Tingjian stood out. He shaped his own calligraphic style with his aesthetic taste and artistic style close to Zen, and his attainments of Zen, creating a distinctive "Zen calligraphy". The success was unmatched by either calligraphers in the Jin (265-420), Tang, Yuan, and Ming (1368-1644) dynasties or his contemporary masters such as Su and Mi. This is also why the "Zen calligraphy" of Huang Tingjian, as a special type in Chinese calligraphy, is particularly irreplaceable

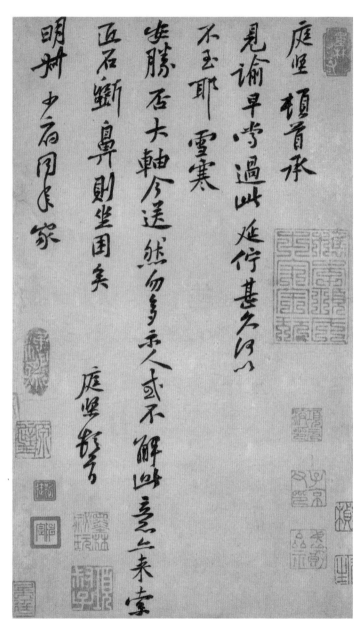

Huang Tingjian's *Xuehan Tie*, collected in Taipei Palace
Museum

Ru Tie (published in Ruzhou) is one of the best-preserved large rubbing collections in China. In China's calligraphic art treasure, *Ru Tie* is one of the best among the ancient stone inscriptions. During the Ming and Qing dynasties (1368-1911), *Ru Tie*, *Quan Tie*, *Jiang Tie*, and *Tan Tie* were called the four famous rubbings. Cheng Wenrong, a famous researcher of steles and rubbings in the Qing Dynasty (1616-1911), spoke highly of it and said

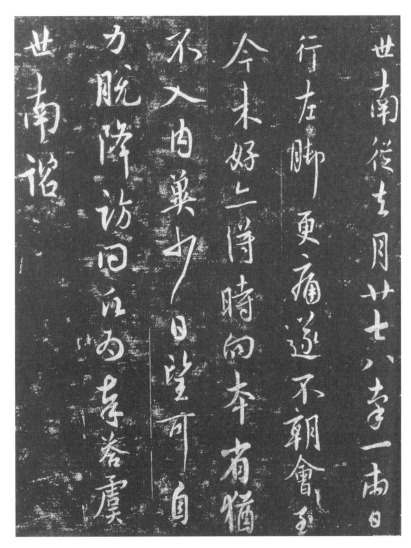

Yu Shinan's cursive writing *Quyue Tie Rubbing*, once included in *Ru Tie*

that it was "a real treasure among stele inscriptions of the Song Dynasty (960-1279)".

1. *Ru Tie* has 12 volumes in total and the content is an individual one. The volumes are as follows: Volume I , bronze inscriptions of three generations; Volume II , stone inscriptions from the Qin and Han Dynasties and Three Kingdoms period (221B.C.-280); Volume III, the calligraphic works of Emperors from the Jin, Song, Qi, Liang, and Chen five Dynasties (265-589); Volume IV, nine calligraphers' works from the Wei and Jin Dynasties (220-420); Volume V , three versions of *A Long Scroll of Letters Beginning with "Seventeen"*; Volume VI, rubbings from Wang Xizhi and Wang Xianzhi, and *On the Goddess of Luo River*; Volume VII, ten calligraphers' works from the Southern Dynasties (420-589); Volume VIII, twelve ministers' works from the Northern Dynasties (386-581); Volume IX, the calligraphic works from four emperors of the Tang Dynasty (618-907); Volume X , the calligraphic works of Ouyang Xun, Yu Shinan, Chu Suiliang, and Xue Ji; Volume XI, six ministers' works of the Tang Dynasty; Volume XII, seven calligraphers' works from the Tang Dynasty to Five Dynasties (907-960). They are calligraphic works from 77 calligraphers and there are also another 23 styles of calligraphy that people can not recognize.

Ru Tie was inscribed by Wang Cai (1078-1118) of the Northern Song Dynasty (960-1127) in the third year of Daguan (1109). Wang Cai, style name (*zi*) Fudao, was from Fuyang, Jiangzhou (now De'an county, Jiangxi), the youngest son of Wang Shaozhi who was a militarist of the Northern Song Dynasty. There is an essay added to the Volume 328 *Wang Shao* in *History of Song*:

Wang Cai, style name (*zi*) Fudao, was fond of learning and writing poems and essays...In the second year of Chongning (1103) when he was 26, he became a *Jinshi* (advanced scholar, a graduate who passed the triennial court exam) and was a civil official in charge of state history...In the third year of Daguan (1109) when he was 32, he was Governor of Ruzhou, and inscribed *Ru Tie*. In the sixth year of Zhenghe (1116) when he was 39, he was Hanlin Academician and Deputy Minister of Military and visited Zituan Mount in Shanxi Province. In the eighth year of Zhenghe (1118) when he was 41, he was incriminated by a false god appearance case and put to death.

Wang Cai explained the reasons to inscribe *Ru Tie* at the end of it:

During the past year when I was in charge of Ruzhou, the local officials and people had lived with my carelessness with government affairs. They did not often ask me for help. So I was alone and leisurely. Besides taking care of my parents, I managed to collect nearly a hundred calligraphers' works by accident from Xia (2070B.C.-1600B.C.), Shang (1600 B.C.-1046 B.C.) and Zhou (1046 B.C.-256 B.C.) Dynasties to Five Dynasties (907-960), including almost all the writing styles: the ancient characters of Cang Jie, *zhuanshu* (seal script), *lishu* (clerical script), *caoshu* (cursive script), *kaishu* (regular script), and *xingshu* (semi-cursive script). I inscribed these rubbings on 12 stones and put them beside the wall of "Zuo Xiao Tang", the local official residence. These inscriptions involved topics on war and peace and the difference of gentlemen and villains. All of them conveyed deep meanings. Those who knew ancient characters and calligraphy called it history of calligraphy, because scholars studying on language and characters focused on not only writing methods but also meanings of ancient characters. Wang Cai of Fu Yang wrote in early August of the third year of Daguan (1109).

Ru Tie was embedded in the wall of "Zuo xiao tang" after it was finished. Later it was moved to the wall of "Wang song lou" (a sightseeing building in the backyard of "Zuo xiao tang"). According to *Ru zhou zhi* (Record of Ruzhou) of Wang Xiongben of the Ming Dynasty (1368-1644), the 12 steles of *Ru Tie* were still well preserved in the first year of Zhengde (1506). During the years of Jiajing (1522-1526), Wang song lou was destroyed and *Ru Tie* was buried in ruins.

In the seventh year of Shunzhi of the Qing Dynasty (1650), Fan Chengzu (a local official) made a wide search and found the stone steles of *Ru Tie*, which were already obscure and unreadable. So the stone steles were renovated and poems were added. Another two stones were inscribed, making the group members become 14. The new *Ru Tie* was moved to the wall of a hotel.

In the eighteenth year of Daoguang (1838), Bai Mingyi, minister of Ruzhou, saw that the original writings were already obscure and many words could no longer be recognized, so he spent a lot of money in buying a rubbing of the original *Ru Tie*. He had some excellent workers re-inscribe the steles, which took them two years. The latest edition was put left of the Ruzhou's official residence and a house was built to protect it. Therefore, the stones of *Ru Tie* were 26 in total: 12 original stones, two added by Fan and twelve re-inscribed by Bai.

From the late Qing Dynasty to the liberation of Ruzhou (1947), the Ruzhou's official residence was destroyed and stele stones were lost. Later the county cultural center made great efforts to search for them and found 16 stones in total from different locations, including the original stones and those re-inscribed by Bai Mingyi. Besides, another four new stones were inscribed and all of them were collected in *Wen miao da cheng dian* (Hall of Great Achievements at the Temple of Confucius) in Ruzhou. Now the stones are in the west hall. The twenty stones were embedded in the north wall and the west wall and were put in two rows vertically. The stele stones of *Ru Tie* have passed through nine hundred years and they now exist as the only remaining original stele stones of the Song Dynasty.

2. There were rubbings of *Ru Tie* from each dynasty since the Song Dynasty. According to *Zhong zhou jin shi ji* of Bi Yuan of the Qing Dynasty, *Ru Tie* was placed in the Wang Song Lou, but "there were many people copying it which caused trouble for the officials". Rubbing is an exact reproduction of stele stones. Now I will talk about the features of rubbings of different periods according to *Comments on Ru Tie and Related Questions* (*Wenbo*, the second edition, 2001) by She Yanyan.

Not many of rubbings of *Ru Tie* from the Song Dynasty have survived. Now there are collections in Shanghai Museum and Palace Museum and Southern Song rubbing that Zhang Yansheng has collected. Generally the rubbings from the Song Dynasty have the following features: (1) The whole rubbing keeps complete and clear characters; (2) The character "Shang" in "Shang qi shi", the title of the third rubbing in the beginning, is well preserved (there is damage in later Song copies); (3) The character "Zhou" in "Zhou qi kuan shi", the title of the fourth rubbing in the beginning, is well preserved; (4) The writings of *Zu chu wen* (essay written to curse the state of Chu), the ninth rubbing in the beginning, are clear and full; (5) The stone rubbing of Suo Jing in Volume IV is complete; (6) The character "xun" in the title of Volume VIII is partially damaged.

Probably the rubbings from the Yuan Dynasty (1206-1368) are the same with those from the Song Dynasty so that stele scholars and authority works of later generations have few accounts of their features.

Generally the features of the rubbings from the Ming Dynasty (1368-1644) are summarized according to the accounts of Weng Fanggang: (1) The character *"xie"* in *"tian lu bi xie"* in the twelfth rubbing of Volume II was relatively complete before the seventh year of Jiajing (1528) but later the left middle part of the character was damaged and looked like the character "gang"; (2) The rubbings of Suo Jing in Volume IV were still complete in the early Ming Dynasty but there were many fractures; (3) The character "xun" in Dao zhao tie by Fan Xun in Volume VIII was damaged and looked like character "tui". The fake *Jiang tie* and *Xing feng lou tie* were both inscribed as "tui" so that the writer became "Fan Tui"; (4) Most of the first half of *Yao shun tie* by Guo Zhongshu in Volume XII was well preserved but the latter part got damaged. The characters of *Zu chu wen* in the beginning were slim.

The rubbings from the Qing Dynasty are unclear because the original stones are seriously damaged. In the seventh year of Shunzhi (1650), the stones had already become obscure and unreadable and the rubbings from the late Qing Dynasty were even worse and almost blank. Therefore, the rubbings from the Qing Dynasty could not reflect the original look of *Ru Tie*. The copy rubbings have kept complete contents, like those inscribed by Bai Mingyi in the Daoguang period (1821-1850).

All in all, there are rubbings of *Ru Tie* from the Song Dynasty to the Qing Dynasty, with original and copied ones existing together.

3. *Ru Tie* has a relatively high value as history material. It has an extremely rich content, including 28 characters created by Cang Jie, an official historian of the Yellow Emperor (2717B.C.-2599B.C.); orders issued by ruler of the Xia Dynasty (2070 B.C.-1600 B.C.); sacrifices of Emperor of the Shang Dynasty (1600 B.C.-1046 B.C.); orders for military actions by Emperor of the Zhou Dynasty; book titles inscribed by Emperor Xuan of Zhou (ruling from 827 B.C.-782 B.C.); *Zu chu wen* by Wu Xian in the Warring States Period (475B.C.-221B.C.); family education of Li Si of the Qin Dynasty (221 B.C.-206 B.C.); Zhuge Kongming's (during Three Kingdoms Period) essays on yin/yang; Emperor Wu of Liang of the Northern Dynasties (386-581) consulting a herbalist doctor; dream records of Tuoba Xiu, Emperor Xiaowu of the Northern Wei Dynasty (386-534); orders of Emperor Yang of the Sui Dynasty (ruling from 604-618); poems by Wu Zetian (ruling from 690-705) after a night banquet in early spring; Ouyang Xun teaching calligraphy; Yu Shinan's appreciation of the Emperor's copy of Wang Xizhi's calligraphy; Chu Suiliang' appreciation of cultural relics; Liu Gongquan praising fruits others give him; Li Huailin's essays on Laozi, Zhuangzi and Kongzi (Confucius), and many other topics. All the contents from the Yellow

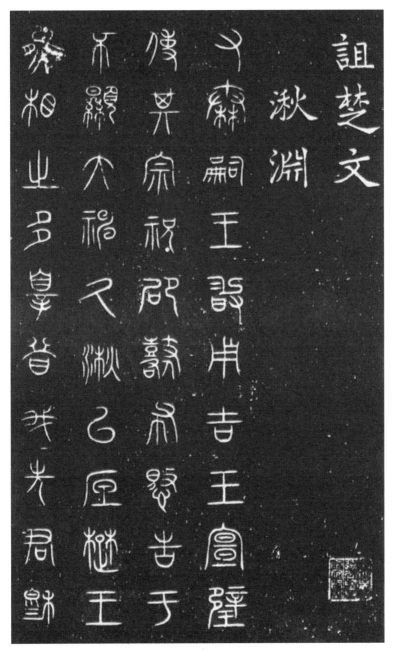

Zu chu wen carved in *Ru Tie*

Emperor to the Five Dynasties, even just several words, are valuable materials. Modern stele scholar Lin Zaiping makes comments on *Ru Tie*, which are as follows:

The source of some contents is nowhere to be known and the original scripts are lost. It is *Ru Tie* that has helped many valuable materials to pass down. For example, both *Feng bi gan mu tong pan* (epitaph of Bigan) and *Zong zi shi shou* (stone animals in front of the tomb of Zong Zi) have been re-inscribed according to *Ru Tie*. Liu Youding learned from Zhuge Wuhou's work and made notes to *Yanji*. Zhang Tianru's *Wang Youjun ji* (Wang Youjun series) also borrowed something from *Ru Tie*. The five-character poem of Last Ruler Li (ruling from 961-976) of the Southern Tang Dynasty and the seven-character poem of Qian Liu, Emperor of Wu Yue (during the Five Dynasties) learned from *Ru Tie* as well. The *Bao zhen zhai fa shu zan* (The Glorification of Bao Zhen Zai's Calligraphy) of Yue Ke recorded that *Xiare Tie* (A Letter Written in Hot Summer) was lack of words and could borrow from *Ru Tie*. This is why ancient inscriptions are so valuable.

The famous scholar of ancient languages Rong Geng wrote a postscript for the *Rubbing of Ru Tie from the Song Dynasty* (kept in Palace Museum), which was:

Zu Chu Wen of the Qin Dynasty was discovered during the Song Dynasty, which was only recorded by *Jiang Tie* and *Ru Tie*. The *Gu shi ke shi ling* (Some

Ancient Stone Inscriptions) I wrote included rubbings of *Ru Tie* from the Ming Dynasty, which were not as good as those from the Song Dynasty. *Zhi fu shi ke* (The Stone Inscription on Zhifu Mount) was only recorded in *Ru Tie*. The *Qin shi huang ke shi kao* (Research of Stone Inscriptions by Emperor Qin Shihuang) I wrote included rubbings from the Qing Dynasty, which were nothing as good as *Ru Tie*. The rubbings of *Ru Tie* from the Song Dynasty were believed to be the worst but I held a different opinion. Ancient people said that "the fewer people know about me, the more valuable I am", because the truly treasure was not necessarily appreciated by the public. Sir Zhu Yu, please take care of it and do not give it to others easily. If I am to reprint my book, I will borrow it from you.

Lin and Rong fully affirmed the significant value of "*Ru Tie*" in Chinese history, literature history, calligraphy history, and the history of Chinese characters research. "*Ru Tie*" has a fairly high value in calligraphic art. The character number of each rubbing varies. The rules and layout are very exquisite, including *zhuanshu* (seal script), *lishu* (clerical script), *kaishu* (regular script), and *caoshu* (cursive script) and many schools. Bronze inscription: round, full, simple, bold, and natural; Stone drum inscription: repeated, peculiar, powerful, and imposing; small seal script: plump and solid; *lishu*: rectangular, vigorous, and simple; *Zhangcao* (early form of cursive script which is based on clerical script): bold and elegant; *kaishu*: square, precise, primitive, and graceful; *caoshu*: unrestricted and elegant. The calligraphy of Emperor Taizong (ruling from 626-649), Wu Zetian and Emperor Xuanzong (ruling from 712-756) of Tang Dynasty is bold and natural; The writing styles of Ouyang Xun, Yu Shinan, Chu Suiliang and Xue Ji in the Early Tang Dynasty and later Li Yong, He Zhizhang, Yan Zhenqing, Han Yu, Liu Zongyuan, Pei Xiu, Yang Ningshi, Li Yu, and Guo Zhongshu, though various and peculiar, are all amazing. *Ru Tie* is a Chinese calligraphic art museum treasured by art lovers in all generations. The Volume I of *Kuai yu tang ti ba* (Annotations of Kai Yu Tang) by Wang Wenzhi of the Qing Dynasty recorded that:

Most reviewers believe that *"Ru Tie"* ranks last among all the rubbings in the Song Dynasty. But there are many fakes and it is difficult to distinguish. *Ru Tie*, which is not very popular, almost has no fakes. Now if you read and appreciate *Ru Tie*, you will find all the merits that the popular *Jiang Tie* and *Tan Tie* cannot compare. Probably this is the difference between genuine works and fake ones...I once said that there were good copies, including both precise and random ones. And *Ru Tie* is one of the latter, so is the recent wood carving *Xi hong tong*. I will not easily say those words if it were not to Bi Yuan, a distinguished scholar in identification of antiquities.

Wang Wenzhi classifies *Ru Tie* into the "crude yet

vivid" category. "Crude" is not rough, sloppy or dull but vigorous, bold, natural, and simple. Looking at the rubbings in history, we can see that there are many precise and vivid scripts and few crude and vivid ones. Zhang Boying speaks highly of Wang Wenzhi's comments: "The comments show great insight. Only those who are proficient in calligraphy can make such comments." He also makes impartial evaluation:

There have been not many rubbings since the ancient times and only the stele stones of *"Ru Tie"* have been completely preserved. It might be a normal object in the Song Dynasty but it is surely a precious treasure today. People of the Song Dynasty were quite good at inscribing and carving but *Ru Tie* was roughly made, just as Huang Bosi (courtesy name: Changrui) said. But there are many excellent works in *Ru Tie* and the stele stones are very elegant. Their vigorousness and solemnity cannot be surpassed by later generations. (Rong Geng, *Collections of Rubbings* I, Chung Hwa Book Co. H.K., 1980, P119)

Wang and Zhang not only spoke highly of the *"Ru Tie"* status in the history of Chinese rubbing research but also fully affirmed its artistic value in calligraphy.

Ren Xun, a Calligrapher of Jin Dynasty

Yin Baoli

Ren Xun (about 1122-1193), courtesy name Junmo (or Junmou), scholar name Nanlu or Longyan, came from Yizhou. He qualified the imperial examinations in the second year of Zhenglong (1157) and served the court in the periods of Hailing, Shizong and Zhangzong. Ren Xun was unfortunate in his official career, while he was skillful in poetry, calligraphy and painting. Above all, his calligraphy was honored as "the best of that time" according to *History of Jin Dynasty•Literary Biography*.

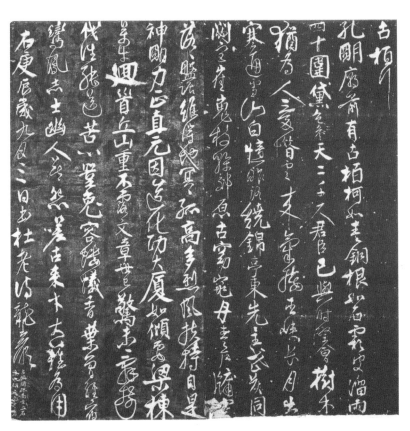

Ren Xun's cursive writing of *A Song of An Old Cypress* by Du Fu

Zhao Binwen of the Jin Dynasty praised Ren Xun's calligraphy that it was magnificent and prosaic. Zhao Binwen used Du Fu's poem as a metaphor and said in Du Fu's poem "How then to describe that Height of Heights? Its verdant landscape engulfs the lands of Qi and Lu.", and the line "How then to describe that Height of Heights?" are even difficult to be called as a simple term, but without the lines the grand writing style of the whole poem would not exist anymore. If the first line is grand too, then it is just the same as Li Changji's writing style. This is forefathers' discussion about poem, so do for calligraphy. The person who wants to learn from Ren Xun should refer to this.

Yuan Haowen of the Jin dynasty appreciated Ren Xun more in the 20th volume of *After Inscribing Nanlu's Calligraphy* of *Collected Works of Fu Shui Idle Old Man*. "The people who are famous for calligraphy in the past century are usually the good forefathers, such as Yuwen Shutong of the imperial academy, Wang Wujing of the Ministry of Rites, Prime Minister Cai Bojian and his son, Wu Yangao, and Gao Ziwen. Yuan Haowen also described the feature of Ren Xun's calligraphy: the handwriting of Ren Nanlu is similar to an experienced judge to try cases in a logic, and clear mode. If let him to govern Jingzhao, he should be comparable with the performance of Zhao Guanghan, Zhang Chang, and Wang Zun, Wang Zhang and Wang Jun."*(Postscript to Famous Calligraphic Works,* the 40th volume of *Complete Works of Yuan Haowen*) *Postscript to Biaohai Ting Poem Stele of Ren Xun* written by an anonymity of the Jin Dynasty said, "Ren Xun is an extraordinary talent. People only know he is a master of calligraphy and honored as 'the Best in the world', but in fact, he was not only good at calligraphy...He is loyal to the country, clean and upright in ruling. If he is not an extraordinary talent, how could it be possible that he did so well than others in riding and shooting, music, painting and calligraphy?" (*Postscript to Biaohai Ting Poem Stele of Ren Xun*, the 49th volume of the Best Jin Wen written by Zhang Jinwu of Qing dynasty) an anonymity admired him very much, "All masters passed away, such as Han Yu and Liu Gongquan, Su Shi and Huang Tingjian, but we fortunately have Ren Xun in the world." (*Zhongzhou Collected Works*, the 2nd volume of Ren Xun, *Complete Library in Four Branches of Literature*, Wenyuange Edition).

Poet Wang Yun of early Yuan Dynasty had collected some calligraphic and painting works of Ren Xun, believing his calligraphic style between Yan Zhenqing of the Tang dynasty and the Su Dongpo of Song dynasty, "Most of Ren's calligraphic works are collected in the capital, and his calligraphic works usually look grave and solemn. While this work is different from others, it is vigorous and unrestrained"(Postcript to Ren's Midnight Crow Inscription , the 71st volume of Epilogue of Autumn

Ravine written by Wang Yun of Yuan Dynasty)

In *Collection of Calligraphic Works* (*Mo Chi Yuan Hai*), the 36th volume of *Peiwenzhai Studio's Encyclopedia of Calligraphy and Paintings* written by Sun Yueban et al. of the Qing Dynasty, it praised Ren Xun's handwriting, "Ren's handwriting is comparable with the two Wang's, Wang Xizhi and Wang Xianzhi of Eastern Jin Dynasty."In the 12th volume of Ma Zonghuo's *Calligraphy Chronicle* (*Shu Lin Zao Jian*), it quoted from the *Pleasure of Ink*, saying that Ren's calligraphy was better than Yan Zhenqing in some aspects, and his *xingcao* (semi-cursive script) is different from Su Shi and Mi Fu.

While it is a big pity that Ren Xun, as a great literary master, had only a few works handed down, including ten poems, three articles but no painting work. As I know, only six of Ren Xun's stone inscription works have been founded by far, which shows the graceful bearing of a great calligrapher.

1. *Gu Bai Xing Shi Bei* (The *Stele of A Song of An Old Cypress*). The Stele was made in the 5th year of Zhenglong (1160), and now is kept in Stele Forest of Xi'an of Shaanxi province, and the National Library also collects the stone rubbings made during the reign of Emperor Qianlong.

2.*Qiu Huai Shi Bei* (*The Stele of Autumn Thoughts Poem*), made in the first year of Dading (1161). In the attached eight lines of engraved text Qi Gong's book of

Quatrains about Chinese Calligraphy (Life, Reading, New Knowledge Joint Publishing, 1999, page 147), the first four lines are the last four sentences of the 11th poem in the *Autumn Thoughts Poem* written by Han Yu of Tang Dynasty, and the last four lines are the preface and postscript written by Ren Xun. The *Autumn Thoughts Poem* is a five-character antiquity with about six hundred characters and the original stone rubbing must be a huge project. It is an early work of Ren Xun. Seeing from chirography, *Autumn Thoughts Poem* and *A Song of An Old Cypress* are in both *kaishu* (regular script) and *caoshu* (cursive script). *Kaishu* is similar to Yan's (Zhenqin), and *caoshu* is similar to Mi (Nangong), imposing, forthright and sincere.

3. *Lyu Jun Mu Biao*(the *Gravestone of Lyu Zheng*), made in the 7th year of Dading(1167), was unearthed in the south bank of Liangshui River in Fengtai District, Beijing in 1991, and now is stored in The Liao and Jin City Wall Museum in Beijing. This stone is still well preserved and all in *dakai* (large regular script). He was in his prime with mature skills then. His work is similar to and better than Yan Zhenqing's, neat and integrated as an experienced judge in case trial. It is one of the best works of Ren Xun.

4. *Da Tiangong Si Bei* (*The Stele of Tiangong Temple*), was made in the 20th year of Dading (1172). Zhao Shu wrote the article and wrote (in red ink) for

167

Lyu Jun Mu Biao(the Gravestone of Lyu Zheng) by Ren Xun, collected in The Liao and Jin City Wall Museum in Beijing

the stone inscription. The stele was in Fengrun County, Hebei. The editor of it was a famous talent at that time. It contains thousands of characters which are all in *dakai* of Yan style, vigorous and mature.

5. *Wanyan Xiyin Shendao Bei* (*The Tablet for Wanyan Xiyin's Tomb Passage*), made in the first year of Dading (1161). It originally stood in the family cemetery of Wanyan Xiyin, in Shulan county of Jilin. This tombstone was built according to the imperial order. Its content was written by Wang Yanqian, a *zhuangyuan* (the best one in the palace exam) during the period of Huangtong, and then rose as a *hanlin scholar*. Ren Xun had been over fifty years old when he wrote the inscription. It contains over two thousand characters, orderly and delicate. But the stone was broken and gradually weathering since Emperor Guangxuan's resign. In 1960s, it was blasted, so the famous stele with rich historical and artistic smell was destroyed completely. In Jilin City's Library and Jilin Provincial Museum, both store its rubbings. His characters inherited Yan Zhenqing's rigid and vigorous style.

6. *Biaohai Ting Shi Bei* (*the Stele of Biaohai Ting's Poem*), a five-character poem with four rhyme, written by Ren Xun in the late period of Dading. Now it is only twenty-nine characters, stored in the South gallery of Fan'gongting Park in Qingzhou of Shandong province. There are related records *in Yidu jinshi ji* (*Inscription of Yidu*) written by Duan Songling of Qing Dynasty. "The

Biaohai Ting Shi Bei(The Stele of Biaohai Ting's Poem, Partial)

part below is missing and the remaining is three feet and one inch in height and width. Each line has six characters and each character's diameter is four inches, five-character poem with four rhymes. The majestic strokes are quite familiar to those of Mi Nangong (Mi Fu). The word diameter of the inscription is seven or eight inches, elegant and cute. Much compliment speech in it, like a postscript for other's poem. The poem and inscription are all in *kaishu* (regular script), without the name and dynasty, but guessed written by Ren Xun." In his *Reserch on Remnant*

Stele of Biaohai Ting's Poem—Calligraphy Art Treasures of Jin Dynasty Found in Qingzhou of Shandong, Li Sen published rubbings of the remnant stele (Northern Heritage, 2004, 3), so that we have the opportunity to see Ren Xun's handwriting in his old age. It is a treasure of Chinese ancient calligraphy and provides a valuable information for studying calligraphy of the Jin Dynasty.

As described above, Ren Xun has written countless works in his life, and was praised by the ancient calligraphers of many dynasties. His reputation spread through the whole imperial court. Despite many of his handwriting were damaged or lost, but with some rubbings, we can still approach the art gallery established by the sage of calligrapher of 800 years ago and see his deep connotation.

Zhao Mengfu and His
Calligraphy in Zhao's Style

Liu Tao

Zhao Mengfu (1254-1322), with the courtesy name Zi'ang and the scholar name Songxue Taoist, was born in Wuxing (now Huzhou), Zhejiang province. His achievements in art, especially in calligraphy, have been well known for several hundred years. His calligraphy in Zhao's style is still popular with many people until now.

Born in the late Southern Song Dynasty (1127-1279), Zhao Mengfu is a descendant of the fourth son of Emperor Taizu of the Song Dynasty (927-976). He is talented although living a pampered life since childhood. "When he didn't come of age at 20, his words had surprised the Confucian scholars in the town. Growing older, people from far places came to ask for his essays with large sum of money" (Dai Biaoyuan, *The Preface to the Songxue House Collection*). He "could recite after reading, and create passages once hold the writing brush" (*History of Yuan Dynasty, Biography*). At the age of 14, he was granted inherited military adviser. The Southern Song Dynasty perished when he was about 20 years old. Kublai Khan established Yuan Empire (1271-1368) and unified China. In Early Yuan Dynasty, Mongolia noble advocated warrior spirits while the status of scholars in the Han nationality was extremely low. Just as the so-called "the ninth class is Confucian scholar and the tenth is beggar" (people were divided into ten classes from the superior to the inferior in Yuan Dynasty), the status of scholars is slightly higher than that of beggars. "Nanren (people of the perished South Song Dynasty)" is listed as the most humble group in Yuan Dynasty. With the double identities of "scholar" and "Nanren", Zhao's status can be easily imagined. At this period, he lived in seclusion at his hometown and devoted himself to poems, calligraphy and painting as entertainment to pass the time. Meanwhile, he laid foundation on art for his later life.

In order to ease ethnic tensions and win over Han

Zhao Mengfu's *On the Goddess of Luo River On the Goddess of Luo River*

scholars, Kublai khan sent Censor Cheng Jufu to "visit talents of the former dynasty" in 1286. Among the 20 talents or so recommended by the censor, Zhao Mengfu ranked first. In the same year, Zhao paid a formal visit to Kublai khan and began his official career. Because of his "brilliant literary temperament", talents in poetry, calligraphy, paintings, etc., and the political ideas and vision, Kublai khan appreciated him very much and assigned him as scholar official, manager of Ministry of War, and later scholar officer in Talent Institution (managing classic works). From the successive five reigns from Shizu (1260-1294) to Yingzong (1321-1323) of the Yuan Dynasty, he was much appreciated. Due to illness, he passed away in 1322. Yingzong gave him the title of "Duke Wei" with the posthumous title of Wen Min. So the later generations also call him "Zhao Wenmin".

These experiences influence Zhao's art career. As an imperial descendant of Song Dynasty, he could enjoy the privilege as a palace noble. In Song Dynasty, only the

emperor and his minister were eligible for inscription on paintings, so was him. In Yuan Palace, he brought it to the literati around, gradually making painting inscription a tradition. "Poetry, calligraphy and painting skills gathered in one person" was also started by him.

His calligraphy style has changed for three times. At first, he was fond of the calligraphy of Emperor Gaozong of the Song Dynasty (1107-1187), who was both enthusiastic to copy calligraphy models of Jin and Tang dynasties and write *zhangcao* (early form of cursive script which is based on clerical script). Before 40 years old, Zhao Mengfu committed himself to learning *zhangcao* from Gaozong. Figure 1 is his *zhangcao* work *Quick Zhangcao*. From 40 to 60 years old he pursued Wang Xizhi's ancient style. The main content of retro movement that he advocated is to restore the status of Wang Xizhi's calligraphy style. People in Yuan Dynasty generally followed Zhao, and abandoned the calligraphy style of pursuing connotation, which made Zhao the leader in calligraphy field of Yuan Dynasty. At this stage, he got "the only ancient copy" *of Dingwu Lanting*. He seemed to have found out treasure, and repeatedly imitated it. After making many prefaces and postscripts, he wrote the famous *The Thirteenth Postscript of Lanting* (Figure 2). From this calligraphy work we can see clearly that he inherited Wang Xizhi's style in the work of *Lanting Preface*. At old age, namely after the Yanyou (1314-1320) period, he turned to studying the calligraphy of Li Beihai and Liu Gongquan in Tang Dynasty (618-907) and changed his style again. The popular works at this stage include *dakai* (large regular script tomb inscriptions draft) such as *Chou'e Tomb Inscription* (Figure 3), *Record on Repairing Sanmen Gate of Xuanmiao Taoist Temple* (Figure 4), *xiaokai* (small regular script) such as *Memoirist on Ji'an in Han Dynasty* (Figure 5), in which the *Record on Repairing Sanmen Gate* is rated by Li Rihua as "Zhao's stele ranks first in the world" (*Comment on Calligraphy*). His *Inscription on GuiZhuang Painting* (Figure 6) is the typical "Zhao's Style" at this stage.

Song Lian, a famous scholar in early Ming Dynasty (1368-1644), once said: "Zhao Mengfu's calligraphy changes for several times. At the beginning he copied the writing of Emperor Gaozong of the Song Dynasty, and then learnt the styles of Zhong Yao, Wang Xizhi and Wang Xianzhi. At last he focused on the style of Li Beihai," It basically sums up the three changes of Zhao

Mengfu's calligraphy. He mainly wrote *kaishu, xingshu* (running script) and caoshu in these stages. The so-called "Zhao's style" also refers to them, which exert much influence on later generations. In addition, he is also skilled in zhuanshu (seal script), *xingshu* and caoshu. These styles are also important subjects of his retro movement.

Before Yuan Dynasty, zhuanshu, *lishu* and *zhangcao* were neglected and nearly on the brink of extinction. Although Emperor Gaozong of the Song Dynasty wrote *zhangcao*, he failed to make its renaissance. Zhao Mengfu that revived those old styles and made considerable achievements as well. His works in zhuanshu are often seen on tablets, and *lishu* is relatively rare to be found. *The History of Calligraphy* in *Yuan Dynasty* said that he "is famous for his calligraphy in *zhuanshu, zhou* (one of the large seal scripts), *fenshu* (the former style of *lishu*), *lishu, kaishu* (regular script), *xingshu* and *caoshu*", which can be seen from the inside back cover of *The Thousand Characters in Six Styles* (see Vol. 7, 1983 of this journal) that he created at his old age. The retro movement that Zhao Mengfu initiated reestablished the authority of Wang Xizhi's calligraphy, making the calligraphy in Yuan Dynasty present a new look completely different from that in Song Dynasty. For Zhao Mengfu's achievements in this field, many comments have been made by later generations. Especially in the retro movement of Yuan and Ming dynasties, Zhao is regarded as the authority while Su

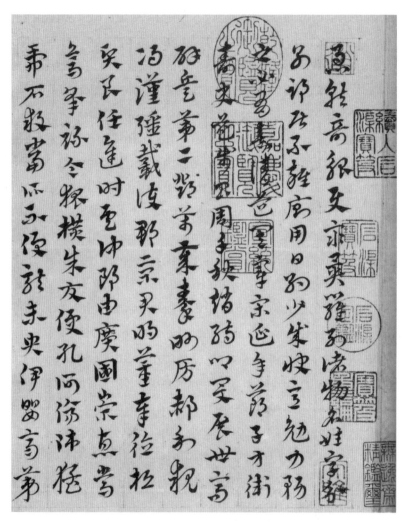

Zhao Mengfu's *zhangcao* work *Hurriedly-written Essay*

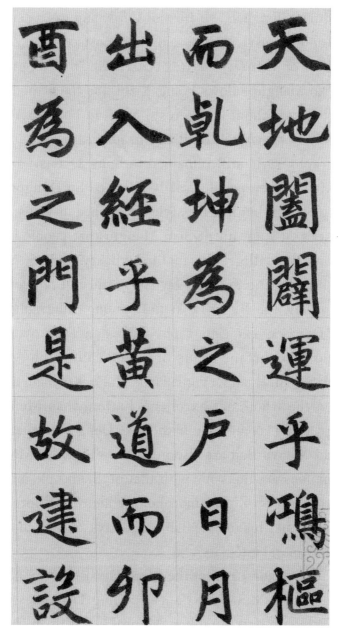

Record on Repairing Sanmen Gate of Xuanmiao Taoist Temple by Zhao Mengfu

Shi, Huang Tingjian, Mi Fu and Cai Xiang as "heterodox ones" and "heresy". Li Kan said in his postscript of Zhao's *On Fault of Qin Dynasty* (221-207 BC): "the calligraphy of Zhao Mengfu follows Wang Xizhi. It's the orthodox in calligraphy without any heresy" Yu Ji in his Dao Yuan's *Record on Studying Ancient Calligraphy* says: "the ancient calligraphy style still remained in Song Dynasty before Cai Xiang. Then people crazily followed Su Dongpo and Huang Shangu but lost the style established in Wei and Jin dynasties...it's not until Zhao Mengfu that people began to learn the calligraphy in Jin Dynasty." Xiang Mu, a calligraphy critic in Ming Dynasty, said in *Comment on Calligraphy*: Cai Xiang ranks first among calligraphers in Song Dynasty. The calligraphy in Qi and Tang dynasties are most important in history. The calligraphy of Li Beihai, Su Shi, Huang Tingjian and Mi Fu is of half heresy and on the whole not excellent. Latter, Zhao Mengfu's calligraphy becomes the orthodox. Deng Wenyuan, Yu He and Xianyu Boji are also good at calligraphy. Most of his opinions are the same with that of the people in Yuan Dynasty. But on Zhao's morphology and moral integrity, Xiang Mu has his own opinions. He says Zhao is "delicate with low moral integrity".

Then, Zhang Chou in the Ming Dynasty and Fu Shan at the end of Ming and the early Qing Dynasties made similar comments on Zhao Mengfu's calligraphy and integrity. Zhang Chou thinks Zhao's calligraphy is "too

fragile and delicate for lack of determined moral integrity".
(*Humble Views of Zhang Chou*). Fu Shan believed Zhao
Mengfu had a humble personality, so his calligraphy was
delicate without any backbone. He drew the conclusion
by relating Zhao's calligraphy taste to his personality. For
Zhao Mengfu, as the imperial descent of Song Dynasty,
finally accepted official positions in Yuan Dynasty, which
is a treachery behavior from the feudal orthodoxy. So he
was regarded as an invertebrate person and that affects
his calligraphy quality. The above are comments from
the perspective of ethics. In addition, the shortcoming
of "Zhao's style" lies in the lack of "personality". Some
people in Ming Dynasty has denounced it as "the slave
of calligraphy". In spite of that, the influence of Zhao's
calligraphy has extended to the Mid-Ming Dynasty when
two calligraphers–Zhu Yunming and Wen Zhengming
were also affected, and even the famous painter Tang
Bohu only wrote *xingshu* in Zhao's style. Since Zhu
Yunming and Wen Zhengming became the leadership
in calligraphy circles, Zhao's status has been gradually
weakened, and then the calligraphy of Dong Qichang
became the most popular one. Due to the preference of the
Emperor Qianlong (1711-1799) in Qing Dynasty (1636-
1912), Zhao's style restored its influence. Liu Yong, who
"made great achievements in rubbing" highly praised
Zhao, and even made a poem to praise him. Meanwhile it
has gradually become the model of "Guangeti (the official

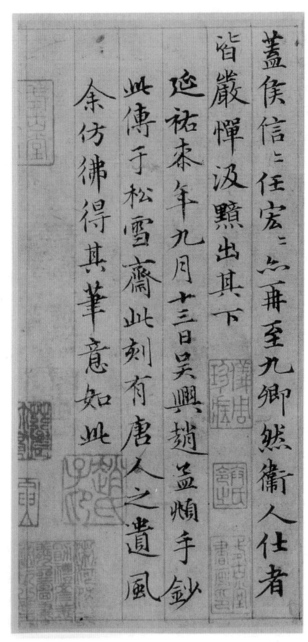

Zhao Mengfu's *Memoirist Biography on Ji'an in Han Dynasty*

style of Qing Dynasty similar to *kaishu*)". So when stele calligraphers such as Bao Shichen, Kang Youwei and so on appeared, the calligraphy of Zhao Mengfu suffered fierce criticism again.

For hundreds of years, there are different comments on Zhao's calligraphy. After all, thanks to his status at that time, lots of his works and inscriptions are passed down. According to Sun Xingyan's record in *Appreciate Steles in the World*, Zhao Mengfu's inscriptions are in an overwhelming majority in Yuan Dynasty. Despite of vicissitudes, we can still see lots of Zhao's authentic calligraphy works now, which, as part of the precious Chinese calligraphy art, still greatly influences later generations. We should envisage and study this calligraphy master and his works, and regard them as the reference and nourishments to explore a new approach to calligraphy art. (Seal cutting: Wang Yun)

On Seal Characters by Wu Changshuo

Chen Zufan

In history of *zhuanshu (seal character)* and *lishu*, it is difficult to find such a model: so purely "old", but also decisively "new". Wu Changshuo—a poor intellectual from a small village, and also a diligent senior with a plain appearance—thoroughly swept away the models of previous dynasties in the history of *zhuanshu* and *lishu*, and formed his unique style of calligraphy, finally becoming an artistic master in the time for new forces rising.

Wu Changshuo's *zhuanshu* copy of *Shiguwen*, collected in Palace Museum, Beijing

Talking about Wu Changshuo's *zhuanshu* and *lishu*, there are praises as well as brickbats. Those who praised such as Fu Tienian and Xiang Shen, said:

Changshuo got his reputation from *shigu* (Stone Drum), and the structure tended to vary, unique and novel.

Changshuo wrote *shiguwen* using Deng Shiru's (a famous calligrapher in Qing Dynasty) technique, brushstrokes changing from horizontally to vertically, forming a separate school. His *shiguwen* is unrestricted, not as meticulous as his *lishu*.

And those who disparaged were as in Ma Zonghuo's *Qiyuelou Bitan (Brush Talk from Qiyue Tower)*:

Changshuo wrote *shigu* with the same way of drawing plum, posing and vigorous, smelling of the country but not implicit, so it had completely broken away from the rule of *lishu*.

At that time, Wu Changshuo just followed his own way, dedicated to the pursuit of *shiguwen*, which evolved from the ancient *jinwen* (bronze inscription) in Warring States period and *zhuanshu* (seal script) developed in Qin Dynasty, and tirelessly devoted all his life to it. As for praises, from either the comment "famous for *shigu*" by Fu Tienian, or Xiang Shen's "writing *shigu* with Deng's technique", we can see a thought of worshiping the ancient, which is a sense of stressing inheritance and the origin of a style. As for what Ma Zonghuo said that "completely broken away from the rule of *lishu*", although Wu Changshuo was discordant with contemporary comments at that time, but his starting point was still based on a traditional criterion. But Ma Zonghuo actually shared a same critical view with Xiang Shen and Fu Tienian, and they all didn't speak to the purpose.

The true value of Wu Changshuo's *zhuanshu* lies not in his *"shigu* learning", which is very superficial, but lies in his study method. From the discussion on *shiguwen*'s historical era, we probably have felt: *shiguwen*, as a kind of character style, is inclined to straighten rigorous *qinzhuan* and has an obvious difference with the changing *jinwen*. Contemporary people will break it in the state of Qin during the Warring States period, and you can know where the message. The style of *shigu*, steady but not extensive enough, should make Wu Changshuo so obsessed that ordinary people could not understand.

I thought it was a tremendous transformation from straightening the original *shigu* to Wu Changshuo's *shigu* calligraphy—from steadiness to unrestrainedness, straightness to discreteness, a vitality of life occurred in the primitive strokes, thus a symmetrical and paralleled structure becomes to irregularity; even lines are changed— the smooth and single lines used by *lishu* calligraphers of previous dynasties, such as Li Si, Li Yangbing and Deng Shiru, were replaced by a kind of powerful lines. In other words, Wu Changshuo found only a few scattered calligraphy "information" from *shigu*. He put these

Wu Changshuo's *zhuanshu* copy *shiguwen*, collected in Shanghai Museum

Wu Changshuo's copy *San Family Plate*

188

meaningful "information" together and re-arranged them with his own wisdom and understanding to create a new "vigor" from the ""old" skeleton. Therefore, we may as well say he's *zhuanshu* style is a "non *shigu*-looking *shigu*".

We say it is *shigu* for its character pattern—*shigu*'s pattern in terms of philology; it is not *shigu*, because in the back of *shigu* hides a Wu Changshuo. We can see that from his writing skills, strokes, character structure, composition and even his writing speed and rhythm. Here, we may also say that to some extent, it is reasonable for Ma Zonghuo to accuse him of "completely broken away from the rule of *lishu*". Wu Changshuo indeed knocked the existed rule of *zhuanshu* since ancient to the ground, showing his unique perspective of choosing.

I think it has a great significance if we can judge Wu Changshuo in a grand history of calligraphy. First, Wu Changshuo's "reform" generated at an atmosphere of pro-skill. If in early *zhuanshu* period from *jinwen* to *qinzhuan*, the calligraphers are still in the stage of free practice but not active to get hold of the artistic style, then they often indulge in a quagmire of pursuing a kind of tiny, narrow, steady or charming style after they are really aware of *zhuanshu*'s artistic value. From the bold and unrestricted *jinwen* to paralleled and meticulous *qinzhuan*, they are all signals with a profound meaning in early history of *zhuanshu*. But during the long process from *zhuanshu*'s turndown in the Tang and Song dynasties to its resurgence

Wu Changshuo's *zhuanshu* of Three Character Couplet

in the Qing Dynasty, there are still many famous *zhuanshu* calligraphers extensively pursuing the pro-skill style. Master Deng Shiru and Zhao Zhijian's *zhuanshu* in that generation are all meticulous and graceful. It is very thought-provoking that the antique calligraphers as Lian Qian and Jia Puxue are all not surprised at this. It is in this graceful atmosphere that Wu Changshuo suddenly rises with a new force; he can easily grab people's hearts with his forceful style, vigorous and deft brushwork as well as disheveled and rough character structure, so that he can get rid of the dilatory and boring style, leading the calligraphic style of the whole time.

Secondly, Wu Changshuo's *zhuanshu* definitely reflects his "Reform" feature of "developing the old into new", "borrowing the previous fire to lighten his own gloom in chest". Different from those in our generation, who study comparative science or Chinese and Western cultures contrast, he would not out rightly oppose to the tradition—innovated based on no tradition. Strictly speaking, his writing skill, composition and brushwork are all "traditional" and also "exclusively innovated". His line is absolutely accord with Chinese traditional aesthetics of thickness, heaviness, power and rhythm; his handwriting is also completely consistent with the principle of classical calligraphy's balance, stagger and interlacing. His calligraphy was not totally new, but has a very strong internal appeal—a strong appeal with an obvious era character—we can even say that its meaning is closely related to the recent and modern ethos; this is a kind of beauty surpassing the classical calligraphy, bold but not inurbane, dignified but not tired.

So we might value Wu Changshuo's *zhuanshu* like that, he was an epoch-making master in the history of *zhuanshu*, and his *zhuanshu* at a higher level symbolized a more successful transformation than other script typefaces, including *lishu*, *xingshu*, *kaishu* and *caoshu*. Its significance is far out of a single script typeface as *lishu*. Only to study his value from such two aspects as the longitudinal history of *zhuanshu* and the horizontal calligraphy history, would we not underestimate his success.

Thousand Character Essay is one of the ancient books for children enlightenment, which has a history of nearly one thousand and five hundred years. It was compiled under the reign of Emperor Wu of the Liang State in the Southern Dynasty. Xiao Yan, the said Emperor Wu of the Liang State, was proficient in literature, calligraphy and many other fields. He highly respected the works of predecessor calligraphers and once praised the work of

Zhongyong's *Thousand Character Essay* in *zhencao*

Wang Xizhi, a famous calligrapher, like "the dragon jumps over the heaven gate, and the tiger crouches in the imperial palace", "all previous dynasties value it and will forever learn from it." To this end, Emperor Wu sent people to get a thousand different characters from his favorite predecessor calligraphers Wang Xizhi and Zhong Yao; and then in the form of four-word rhyme, Zhou Xingsi put them together to form a popular article, which became the well-known *Thousand Character Essay*. According to historical records, the most popular and earliest *Thousand Character Essay* had three versions: one was from Wang Xizhi and Zhong Yao; one was made by Xiao Zifan and another was the rhyming version by Zhou Xingsi. Additionally, Emperor Wu also had his own version of *Thousand Character Essay*. And a variety of sequels and adaptations occurred since Sui Dynasty. According to

Huaisu's *Thousand Character Essay* in *caoshu*

the records in Liang Zhangju's *Landscape Essays* (*Lang Ji Cong Tan*), there was also a *10-Thousand Character Essay* written by Sui Manhui. But only Zhou Xingsi's *Thousand Character Essay* involved the content of nature, society, history, ethics, education and other aspects, good to enlighten the beginners, so it was blessedly handed down.

Zhou Xingsi, courtesy name Si Zuan, from Xiang County, Chen Prefecture, was erudite and good at composition. According to the records of *History of Southern Dynasties*, in the first year of the Tianjian Period of Liang Dynasty, he was appreciated by Emperor Wu for his *Ode to Peace* and therefore was promoted as an assistant minister. And then for his *Ode to Horse*, he was further promoted. Each time he was requested to composite, he would be praised by Emperor Wu. He had written over a hundred volumes of collected works,

including the memoirs about emperors, and served as senior supervising secretary after several promotions. When he was seriously ill, Emperor Wu held his hand and sighed: 'How can a good man contract such a serious disease!" It was Zhou Xingsi's profound literary skills that provided a prerequisite for spreading of *Thousand Character Essay*. And the ancient calligraphers' advocates were also an important factor for the popularizing of *Thousand Character Essay*.

The first transitional celebrity was a Sui Dynasty calligrapher, Dignitary Zhi Yong, who was the seventh generation descendant of Wang Xizhi. According to the Essays after Retirement by Liang Zhangju of the Qing Dynasty, Dignitary Zhiyong lived in Ximing Temple in Chang'an, and he had written *Thousand Character Essay* in *caoshu* for eight hundred times from his seventy to eighty years old. This eight hundred volumes were scattered in different temples in southern China. Qi Gong said in his *Postscript on Japanese Copy of Zhiyong's Thousand Character Essay* that, Japan stored a *Thousand Character*

Thousand Character Essay in *shoujinti* by Zhao Ji, Emperor Huizong of the Song Dynasty

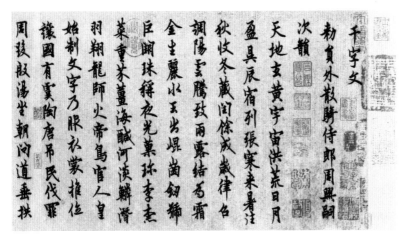

Thousand Character Essay , in *xingshu* by Ouyang Xun

Essay in *Caoshu*, which was brought to Japan in Tang Dynasty. I am sure it was one of the eight hundred copies once collected in various temples of eastern Zhejiang. Dignitary Zhiyong's handwritten *Thousand Character Essay* encouraged generations of calligraphers in a variety of styles and forms to transcript it and also promoted the popularity of our calligraphy.

Several great calligraphers in the Tang Dynasty, such as Huaisu, had written dozens of *Thousand Character*

Essay in total, whose calligraphy was ingenious with the vigor of "an agazed snake into the grass, and blowing smoke more fierce". Huai Su's *Thousand Character Essay in xiaokai* (Small Cursive Script) was the best and was in possession of Wen Zhengming in the Ming Dynasty, and it was world known as *Gold Essay*. Sun Guoting was famous for copying the two Wang's (Wang Xizhi & Wang Xianzhi) hand scripts. His *Thousand Character Essay in caoshu* (cursive script) was inscribed by Wang Xian, a famous calligrapher in Northern Song Dynasties, as posing and peculiar. Ouyang Xun's *Thousand Character Essay* in *kaishu (running script)*" (see inside back cover), bearing harmony with spirit floating down, was the unique copy of Ou's manuscript handed down in the world. Some idle monks specialized in *caoshu* (cursive script) and learned from Zhang Xu and Huai Su, whose extant *Thousand Character Essay* has become fragmentary but its strokes are still "free and natural, forming a unique style." Other calligraphers in the Tang Dynasty, including Chu Suiliang, Zhang Xu, Pei Xingjian, Zhong Shaojing, Monk Biancai, Mengying and Zhao Moji, also wrote *Thousand Character Essay* and their works have been handed down.

By the Song Dynasty, there were Li Jianzhong's *Thousand Character Essay*, Mi Fu's *Thousand Character Essay* in *xiaokai*(small regular script), Wang Sheng's and Wang Zhu's *Thousand Character Essay* in *caoshu* (cursive script) having been passed down. Wang Zhu was a legend person and he became an Academician of Hanlin for he can imitate Wang Xizhi's script. Every time Zhao Guangyi, emperor Taizong of the Song Dynasty, finished his writing, he would always sent to Wang Zhu for comments and hope to get his praise. But Wang Zhu always said the Emperor's writing was not good enough and had to go on practicing. So under such incentive, he took much more efforts on calligraphy, and finally his brushwork got gradually refined. Several emperors in Song Dynasty also loved calligraphy and often practiced *Thousand Character Essay*. Zhao Ji was the last emperor of the Northern Song Dynasty, but he had attainments in calligraphy and painting. The *shoujinti* (thin gold script) created by him was very famous. He copied Ci Tongguan's *kaishu Thousand Character Essay*, whose strokes were thin and rigid, vigorous and upright. His authentic *caoshu* (cursive script), which was handed down, was only the 1st volume of the *Thousand Character Essay* written when he was forty years old, on a thirty-feet long roll, written with one stretch, no tired stroke. Zhao Gou quite liked collecting famous copybooks of previous calligraphers, plus his diligent study on calligraphy, so he had also a volume of *Thousand Character Essay* survived. When he became overlord, once Zhao Shenjin personally wrote *Thousand Character Essay in zhencao* (real cursive script) to celebrate his birthday. He was very happy and praised, "My older brother has gotten a great progress in calligraphy."

(See Zhou Mi's *Old stories from Wulin*)

In Yuan Dynasty, the one who wrote *Thousand Character Essay* most was Zhao Mengfu, a descendant of imperial family of Song Dynasty. He had written *Thousand Character Essay* in two, four and six- character styles. It is said that he had copied Zhi Yong's *Thousand Character Essay* up to five hundred sheets of paper when he was young and could reach the similar level with Zhiyong. This can be confirmed from Wen Zhengming's postscript, "I read it for several days, but it was effected greatly by Zhiyong and nearly has no difference from Zhiyong's." Zhao had also assessed his own *Thousand Character Essay*, which can be found in the *Records of Retirement from Farming*, "I (Mengfu) self-evaluate that I had been writing *Thousand Character Essay* for hundreds of copies during the past twenty years, and this volume was written a few years ago." Because of his great reputation in calligraphy, even the emperor also noticed to collect his works. It is said that in the third year of Yanyou, the Emperor issued edicts that Every time Zhao Zi'ang wrote *Thousand Character Essay*, the book secretary must mount it and store it well. This can also be confirmed in the postscript of Zhao Mengfu's *Thousand Character Essay* written by Zhu Yizun in the Qing Dynasty, *Thousand Character Essay*...many people had written. But in the third year of Yanyou Period, Zhao Zi'ang was requested by the Emperor to write seventeen volumes of *Thousand Character Essay*, and he

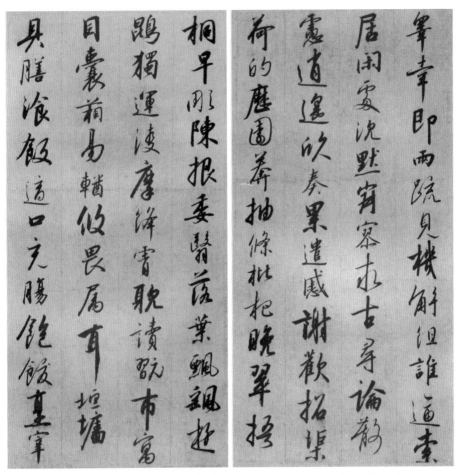

Thousand Character Essay in *xingshu* by Emperor Gaozong of the Song Dynasty

ordered the book monitoring secretary to store them. This may be one of the seventeen volumes. Zhao Mengfu's wife was also a female who was proficient in calligraphy and literature." It can be seen that the couple often copy the *Thousand Character Essay*. Another one good at *xingshu* (semi-cursive script) was a Beijinger, Xianyu Boji, who enjoyed the same reputation with Zhao Mengfu, so there have been a rumor that Zhao was jealous of Xianyu Boji's fame. In fact, Zhao respected Xianyu Boji's script very much, which can not only be proved in history books, but also from their co-written *Thousand Character Essay*. There are also handwritten *Thousand Character Essay* by Jie Xisi, Yu He, Wu Mengsi, Zhao Yong, Bian Wu and so on in Yuan Dynasty surviving in the world.

In Ming Dynasty, the calligrapher and painter, Wen Zhengming wrote *Thousand Character Essay* for the most times. He also started practicing calligraphy by coping it since young. It is said that when he was young, he had to finish writing ten times, so Dong Qichang said it was Wen Zhengming's daily task to copy *Thousand Character Essay*. Wen Zhengming not only wrote *Thousand Character Essay*, but also drew a picture on the back of one hand-roll, which was according to "Ji Qin Ruan Xiao"(Ji Kang was good at plucking a certain musical instrument while Ruan Ji whistling) in the *Thousand Character Essay*. In Ming Dynasty, there were two people of Shanghai wrote *Thousand Character Essay in caoshu* (cursive Script); one was Zhang Bi, a Bingxu scholar of Chenghua, whose stroke was "swift, flying, but well-proportioned". Another was Shen Can, whose work had a feeling of "flying snakes". Cheng Nanyun, who has been involved with the revision of *Yongle Dadian*, Wang Chong, who was as famous as Wen Zhengming, and Dong Qichang, Su Meiyang, Zhou Bowen,

Thousand Character Essay in *xiaokai* by Wen Zhengming

Wen Peng all had *Thousand Character Essay* handed down.

Those *Thousand Character Essay* that had passed down from Qing Dynasty were written by Zhang Yuzhao, an official in Grand Secretariat during the Daoguang period. Modern celebrities such as Zhang Taiyan, Shen Yinmo, artist Huang Binhong had also written *Thousand Character Essay*.

Throughout the past thousand years, the one thousand-character essay has been valued by celebrities of previous dynasties. Lu You, a poet in Song Dynasty, even described that his uncle got enlightened by reading *Thousand Character Essay*, his uncle was over eighty years old, old but not feeble. It can be seen that the ancients did not underestimate the thousand character essay popular regardless it was a book for children

Zheng Banqiao's Calligraphy in the Rubbing *Prices for Art Work*

As one of the "Eight Eccentric Artists" in Yangzhou (in the middle of Jiangsu province), Zheng Banqiao is well known for his skills in poetry, calligraphy and paintings. Especially, his refined and unique calligraphy exerts much influence on later generations. Many people interested in calligraphy always learn from him and imitate his writings, but rare of them can really understand his calligraphy and point out its essentials. So most just copy his works

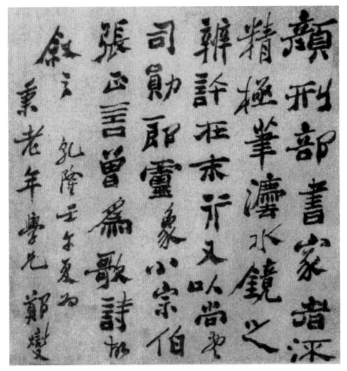

Prices for Art Work by Zheng Banqiao

in Banqiao Style but can't truly master it. Through the analysis of the rubbing *Prices for Art Work*, this article tries to talk about Zheng Banqiao's calligraphy from the individual to the general. Just as an introduction, it offers reference for beginners of Banqiao Style.

Prices for Art Work, also called *Notice on Bidding Farewell*, was written by Zheng Banqiao in the last sixth year (1759) of his life. Because it isn't a serious "red tape" in content but vulgar sketches to have fun for himself, there are no scruples during writing, for which his deep capability, adept skills and the emotional state of mind at the writing moment are all naturally revealed. It's in Zheng Banqiao's work at his twilight years that best embodies his unique charm and style.

It seems difficult to summarize the characteristics of Zheng Banqiao's calligraphy. At the most time people generally refer it with one word--"strangeness". Where does the "strangeness" come from? There are mainly four reasons involved after a careful analysis. They are illustrated taken this rubbing as an example:

1. A mixture of *kaishu, caoshu, lishu* and *zuanshu*. Zheng Banqiao likes to adopt the structures of *dazhuan* (seal style) in some characters or character groups in one work, but writes in xingkai (semi-running script) and *xingcao* (semi-cursive script). For example, the "四(si)" in the second line and the "卯(mao)" in the twentieth line both adopt *xiaozhuan*; the "则(Ze)" in the ninth line, the "神(shen)" in the thirteenth line, and the "语(Yu)" in the fourteenth line adopt *dazhuan*; Strokes of these characters are not all in *xiaozhuan* but with a few xingkai's and *lishu*'s characteristics. Some combine the structure of *lishu* and the characteristic of xingkai, such as the "幅(fu)" in the second line, the "礼(li)" in the sixth line and the "边(bian)" in the twentieth line. Zheng Banqiao often used lishu with characteristic of *xingcao*, or *xingcao* with characteristic of zhuanshu and *lishu*, and sometimes even a mixture of all styles that can't be clearly identified. So if we look at

The horizontal scroll of calligraphy *Ignorance Is Bliss* by Zheng Banqiao

a single character, his calligraphy is strange; but for the consistent changes they are integrated and coordinated on the whole .

2. Take momentum from one side without too much steepness. Zheng Banqiao's *kaishu* and *xingshu* often abandon square structures to pursue steepness. Whether in single or compound characters, he often lowers the left part and uplifts its right, making the lower left corner dark and the lower right corner light. For example, "斗 (dou)" in the fifth line, "食(shi)" in the sixth line, "妙(miao)" in the seventh line, "现(xian)" in the ninth line, and "物 (wu)" in the eleventh line etc. The balance center of these characters moves to the left while the body leans right. The right upper corner is a pointed end, like a flying eaves high in the sky, slant and firm, which presents a unique

courageous and hard-edged posture.

3. Hide skills in seemingly childish strokes. The horizontal right slants such as "送(song)" in the sixth line and "之(zhi)" in the eighth line don't follow the "送" in conventional style in the eighth line but deliberately hide complicated changes, resulting in straight and slightly oblique structures; the "语(yu)" in the eighth line is intentionally designed in disproportion as it is small on the left and big on the right; "论(lun)" in the eighteenth line is intentionally written loosely, plain and unpolished. If we look at these characters in isolation, there are indeed no signs of genius. But they are so coordinated and appropriate seen from their responding relation with the surrounding character groups and the overall composition of various heavy and light rhythms. Besides, these childish strokes are dotted with "strangeness", which avoids pomposity if there are all art skills in the work. Changing into another style (such as square characters) would be too smart. In Zheng Banqiao's calligraphy, there are such "slow-witted" strokes just like that the wisest man often seems stupid beyond mundane sense. They are by no means "casual styles and characters" without any basic knowledge on calligraphy.

4. Increase interest by employ painting skills in calligraphy. Zheng Banqiao "is a talent in both painting and calligraphy. He even combines them", so he could "integrate painting skills in calligraphy, and incorporate

calligraphy techniques into painting". He had once "created calligraphy like willow leaves with a painting brush". Because he was most skilled in painting orchid and bamboo, most of his calligraphy works integrate skills in painting orchid and bamboo intentionally or unconsciously. For example, the end stroke of "也(ye)" in the ninth line adopts the technique of painting bamboo leaves, falling freely and beautifully; the turn slant of "纠(jiu)" in the eleventh line uses the technique of painting bamboo stems, seeming upright and powerful; the last stroke of "也(ye)" in the fifteenth line uses the technique of painting orchid leaves, which is graceful and unrestrained. In this way, he enriches not only the already changeable *xingcao*, as well as the composition but also the taste and interest of the calligraphy.

The above characteristics actually are some special techniques of expression. Are they created by Zheng Banqiao? No. They are adopted by many people in ancient or modern times. For example, Li Yong and Huang Tingjian also took momentum from one side of characters; Mi Fu integrated painting skills into calligraphy; Yi Bingshou and Chen Mansheng combined *lishu* with xingkai. However, the calligraphy style of these people is not known for "strangeness" like Zheng Banqiao. Is it strange? Actually, these people only concentrated on one aspect, but Zheng Banqiao could organically combine various techniques together and naturally incorporate all their strengths in one, so that he not only created his personal calligraphy style, but expressed his complex mood and special personality formed by his experience. People who laugh at Banqiao style as "trifling matter neither belongs to this style nor that class; neither modern nor ancient" really don't know anything about calligraphy. They fail to realize that "calligraphy reflects the character of the writer".

Obviously, "strangeness" is indeed the characteristic of Zheng Banqiao's calligraphy, but it is not comprehensive nor profound enough to sum up his calligraphic art with one word. Because, among many of his xingkai and *xingcao* works, just a few adopt the "strange style" of mixing several expression means. Getting rid of the few "strangeness", we can find that the structure and strokes almost totally follow predecessors' standard. For instance, characters in the rubbing *Prices for Art Work*, such as "两 (liang)", "赊(she)", "赖(lai)" and so on are similar to the calligraphy of Su Dongpo; from characters of "银(yin)", "所(suo)", "缠(chan)" and so on, we can see the calligraphy of Huang Shangu; characters of "为(wei)", "之(zhi)", "高 (gao)" "六(liu)" in caoshu show the style of Wang Xizhi. If we look at Zheng Banqiao's original handwriting of court documents (Mr. Li Yimeng produced a book named *Zheng Banqiao's Court Documents*) written when he was a "petty official", we will not find any "strangeness". Because there was no idea appeared to make the documents

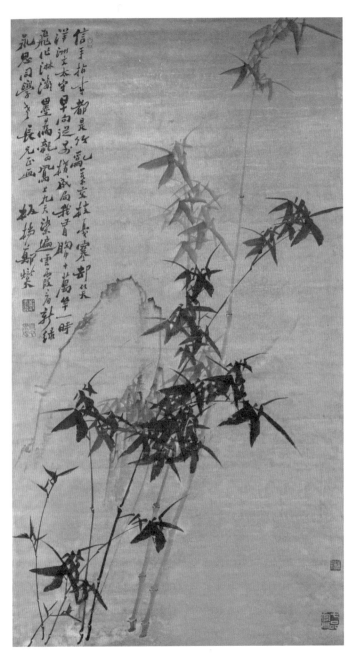

Bamboo and Rock by Zheng Banqiao

popular as calligraphy works, so he didn't elaborately engage in them. All these works are the natural revelation of his capabilities and skills. From the characters that are not "strange", we can see the calligraphy rules of Tang and Song dynasties and the style in Wei and Jin dynasties everywhere. That's the real appearance of Zheng Banqiao's calligraphy without "makeup". Thus we can say Zheng Banqiao's calligraphy works are based on traditional styles with a "strange" appearance. The so-called Zheng Banqiao "doesn't follow the ordinary way" is also deeply rooted in the tradition. This may be the reason that Zheng Banqiao's style is "strange instead of crooked".

The above is just the characteristics of Zheng Banqiao's calligraphy in structure and stroke. The three elements of good calligraphy include structure, stroke and composition. "The composition is most important for a work". On the whole, the composition is the key to a work's success. Zheng Banqiao also showed his ingenuity on the overall layout in his calligraphy. The following is a specific analysis taken *Prices for Art Work* as an example.

There are three prominent characteristics in the composition of *Prices for Art Work*. First of all, it is full of changes as a coherent entity. The total 132 characters in the work are divided into 22 lines with unfixed spacing and length; the beginning of the lines is basically uniform, but the end is rather irregular. The blank space is arranged very boldly. Exaggeratedly, people can even ride a horse in the blank, but even one needle can't get in between the dense part. An extremely strong contrast is presented between the empty and full spaces in the mid-bottom. As for characters in a line, some are a few, some more; some big, some small; some aslant, some upright; some release the stroke, some end the stroke; some are light, some heavy; some skillful and some clumsy. And combined with different structures of the same characters, changeable styles and rhythm etc., his calligraphy applies changes to the highest level. However, there is a natural coordination between the beginning and the end, so it's still an integrated one on the whole picture. Zheng Banqiao once described Mi Fu's calligraphy as "with great dexterity and preternatural swiftness" and "I can't learn, or dare not learn". In fact, he has grasped Mi Fu's essentials well. As of changes, Zheng goes even farther.

Second, the bright rhythm is just like the melody of music. According to different contents, the strokes of the calligraphy work obviously present changes in both strength and speed. The first five lines are about prices for art work, which contain three heavy lines and two light lines. The strokes change from massive and placid style to lively ones, just like the music starts with deep sound and then changes to fast rhythm as a transition. The middle is a "spoken part" to bid farewell to guests, in which the first two lines (the sixth and seventh lines) are heavy, which coordinates with the first two lines in the first part (the fourth and fifth lines), and then the following alternates with heavy and light strokes. The important characters in the sentences are highlighted by changing their style or increasing their size. The strokes in this part are sometimes urgent and sometimes slow with fluctuations, showing a melodious theme. "It sounds like heavy rain when strumming the pipa, and like whisper when flipping it; playing in the two means alternately, it sounds like beads falling into a jade plate". The end part is a poem and his signature. The strength of the first four lines reaches its best proportion. Strokes go on leisurely, like music draws to a closure from the bold and unrestrained rhythm to peace. Suddenly, a large-sized character emerges in the next line like a heavy hammer drums to end the music. The last three lines of small-sized signature are just like the lingering sound with haunting aftertaste.

Third, the momentum reflected by all characters associate with each other. It is discussed in terms of the relationship between the momentum and individual characters. It's a taboo of the composition if the individual character is isolated from the surroundings. Taking a closer look at Zheng Banqiao's individual characters in this rubbing, we can see that they not only have different shapes in height, thickness and dynamic conditions, but also echo each other and look harmonious from top to bottom. So the whole work organically forms an integration. Look at first characters in middle lines: "好(hao)", "心(xin)", "物(wu)",

"欠(qian)", "神(shen)", "诸(zhu)", and "也(ye)". They have very close relation to bow, greet or follow one another. The character "也(ye)" is especially amazing. It dominates one line with two cross strokes, of which the last stroke uses the skill of painting orchids to shape into an arc prolapse. Seen from the right, they seem to raise their head high, following the former half line with characters "诸君子(zhu jun zi)" and so on; Seen from the left, they appear to bow with hands clasped to the line with characters "画竹多(hua zhu duo)". The blank between the two lines is too wide but not separates them as a whole. The blank arrangement is really a miracle as a transition and serves the best example called "coordination between lines"!

This work is neither a general poem scroll nor a common long banner but a specific form with the special content. Zheng Banqiao adopted an unprecedented and unique layout to reach the unique artistic effect. It is unrestrainedly romantic and novel in the calligraphy style, like essays of Zhuangzi and poems of Li Bai. Furthermore, if we link the calligraphy style with the content together, boundless implication and interest can be sensed. Thus, the art of calligraphy also requires highly uniform content and form.

The reason that Zheng Banqiao's calligraphy can "form his own unique style in history" lies in that his capabilities in various aspects. One is the solid foundation in traditional calligraphy. He mastered extensive knowledge of the famous calligraphers from Qin and Han dynasties to Ming and Qing dynasties. Therefore he could "combine all their strengths in each stroke". Secondly, he had a solid foundation on Chinese characters. He was adept in all ancient calligraphy styles of *dazhuan*, caoshu, *zhenshu* and *lishu* as well as strange characters, their deformations, and evolution process. Therefore, he could write freely with all skills as required. Thirdly, Zheng Banqiao was talented in all of the poetry, composition, calligraphy and painting, so he could compose calligraphy work by using painting techniques, integrating poem mood in calligraphy, and creating the profound artistic realm to express his own feelings. Moreover, Zheng Banqiao had faith in Confucius, Laozi, and Zhuangzi, and he was unconventional by nature. So, in calligraphic creation, he respected tradition, but not bounded by it. He made bold innovation and set his own standard. Of course, there are other factors such as his natural endowments and the era background. In a word, the achievements of a master come from extensive knowledge accumulation and long-term special training. They are the necessary preconditions to accomplish the best calligraphy, and integrated embodiment of the cultural competence, art skills, and personal temperament. It's no doubt that a careful study of Zheng Banqiao's artistic practice is beneficial to the inheritance and development of Chinese calligraphy.

Chinese characters are the crystal of the wisdom of Chinese people

It's necessary to know Chinese characters if you want to learn about calligraphy. Since modern times, there has been a misunderstood belief that Chinese characters delay the speed of reading and writing and restrict cultural development. However, with the progress of society and the gradual deepening of research, there is more

A Fan in *lishu* by Ouyang Zhongshi

justification for their use. Now everybody realizes that as a great creation, Chinese characters are the crystal of the wisdom of Chinese people. Among the world's oldest characters, it's only the Chinese that are still in use today. That's because Chinese has a variety of beneficial elements, which enables it to survive until now.

Language is the direct reflection of thinking. Limited by time and space, it needs further development, which turns to characters. As many other early characters from various nationalities, Chinese characters are originated from pictographs.

Xu Shen said "characters are the reflection of things", which are "near from people themselves, and far from all objects". But it's not enough to only have pictographs because some abstract meanings are difficult to demonstrate. Thus the self-explanatory and associative methods and other methods were developed. As the basic word formation principle, the pictograph method conveys meanings through shape descriptions of objects, which enables it to spread in space and time. The emergence of associative characters shows the Chinese people's wisdom. As China covers a vast geographic area, transportation is inconvenient and regional pronunciations cannot be unified. However, there is a feature that most dialects are made of monosyllables. The combination of this feature with pictographs, self-explanatory, and associative led to word-formation methods which have been passed down from an ideographical character system rather than follow phonetic orientation. Our ancestors brilliantly created several components with the method of classification.

What is more, the most representative components are chosen as the prominently typical model to lead almost all the glyphs, which are known as "radicals".

So, although the total number of Chinese characters is large, the basic component of the characters is relatively simple and easy to master. The classified components constitute the ancestors' cognition of the world. So the thought is not only reflected by language but also by the character system: it reflects people's cognition to the world, resulting in both separation and combination conditions of "language" and "character". I think "written language" is not to record "spoken language" directly, but the crystal of "characters".

The Chinese language is a string of gorgeous and glittering beads

Chinese characters boast great flexibility for sentence-making. Classical Chinese is very flexible in word selection without any rules. For example, nominative, accusative, past tense or present tense and so on. Although the meaning is not so clear at first glance, classical Chinese has the advantage of simplicity. At the same time, it will not influence the record and conveying of the overall meaning.

Basically, each Chinese character has one form and one pronunciation. The word property changes flexibly, so it has the advantage of pursuing "orderliness" in form. For example, couplets make the best use of this characteristic with two symmetrical sentences and an ordered form, which can't be found in the Western literature. Our "Modern Style Poetry" (not New Poetry, but poems since the Tang Dynasty poetry, namely metrical poem) has the same characteristic. It has four or eight sentences, unified but not monotonous, with five or seven words in each sentence of the same length. Some figures of speech in poems, Ci (a type of classical Chinese poetry), Qu (a type of verse for singing), and couplets pay attention to connotation, such as the "green" in the verse "spring breeze again and greens the south bank of the Yangtze River" is very vivid and expressive as a verb. Some pay attention to pronunciation, such as "lotus seed is bitter inside; pear is acid in heart", which seems to talk about the

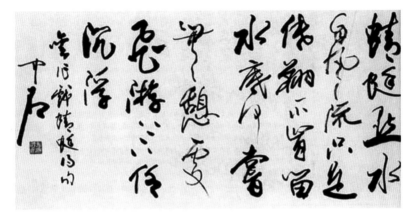

Ouyang Zhongshi's banner works

features of the two fruits, but can also express another layer of meaning, "missing son (the same pronunciation with 'lotus seed' in Chinese) is bitter inside; the left son (the same pronunciation with 'pears' in Chinese) is sad (the same pronunciation with 'acid' in Chinese) in heart", which reflects the feelings of a mother reluctantly bidding farewell to her son.

Some skillfully use the "form" of Chinese characters to develop wonderful and deep content. There is a widely spread antithetical couplet "smoke encircles the willow in the pond; cannonball protects the tower near the sea" (烟锁池塘柳，炮镇海城楼). There seems to be nothing strange, but from the glyph, the corresponding components of each character in the two lines are "fire (火)" "gold (金)" "water (水)" "soil (土)" "wood (木)", the so-called "five elements" in Chinese culture. Some people say that China is a country of poetry. It makes sense. I think "Chinese characters" are the crystal of the wisdom of Chinese people and the Chinese language is a string of gorgeous and glittering beads that connect many crystals orderly.

"Goodness" is the core pursuit of culture

The beautiful "Chinese" is part of the Chinese culture. What is "culture"? According to the dictionary, culture is: "the combination of the material wealth and spiritual wealth that people have created in the process of social and historical practice."

It seems abstract for its all-encompassing nature. But it can be understood well if we think carefully. Xu Shen said: "culture is the interlacement of things", which is similar to "interlacing is culture" *in The Book of Changes*. But only to mix or crisscross is not enough, so *The Book of Rites* says "culture is made up of all kinds of things in order", which is both rich and harmonious. Here, "in order" means "harmony" and "goodness". In the development of the Chinese culture, the Chinese people have not only protected the nation's excellent traditions but also absorbed cultures from others, so the Chinese culture is "made up of all kinds of things". The pursuit for "good" human life is the permanent goal. The combination of the pursuit for "goodness" with everything in the world is "culture".

Calligraphy is a learned skill based on the Chinese culture to manifest cultural beauty

The word "calligraphy" in Chinese refers to the approaches to writing history in the earliest times. It later changed into rules of characters-writing. Now we regard it as a category of art. But as I see it, it is a learned skill.

Some people think calligraphy is the least or trivial skill of scholars. Actually it can solve big problems. Throughout history, how could language be presented without the ability "writing"?

Even now, calligraphy shows people content of the Chinese language in a rhetoric, rhythmic, emotional, and dynamic way. Chinese characters are the crystal of the wisdom of Chinese people. The Chinese language is a string of gorgeous and glittering beads. And then calligraphy is the beautiful aura on the beads.

I always emphasize the relation between calligraphy, Chinese characters and the Chinese language, and ask my students to study calligraphy on the basis of the other two and pay attention to accumulating knowledge on philology, literature, history, archaeology, aesthetics and other subjects.

Once upon a time, I raised the idea that "the core of calligraphy is the Chinese culture", and later changed it into "accumulate knowledge and demonstrate it in a higher level" and then extended it to "culture paves the way for writing and calligraphy as the crystal of the Chinese language sparkling the characters". After some thinking, the fourth sentence was changed into "all our activities should meet the needs of the times".

In the combination of crystal, beads and halo, calligraphy makes it possible for Chinese characters and Chinese language that are loaded with "Tao", an attractive and vivid image to meet the needs of the society, history and era. Calligraphy matters not only in writing good characters, but also in manifesting the "beauty" of culture.

图书在版编目（CIP）数据

名家讲中国书法名作 : 英文 / 《文史知识》编辑部编；杨树青，李慧娇译.
－ 北京 : 五洲传播出版社，2016.1（中国文化经典导读）
ISBN 978-7-5085-3088-8

Ⅰ．①名… Ⅱ．①文… ②杨… Ⅲ．①汉字－书法－介绍－中国
－英文 Ⅳ．①J292.1

中国版本图书馆CIP数据核字(2016)第019118号

名家讲中国书法名作

编　　者：《文史知识》编辑部
翻　　译：杨树青 李慧娇
出 版 人：荆孝敏
责任编辑：王峰
装帧设计：壹东设计
出版发行：五洲传播出版社
地　　址：北京市海淀区北三环中路31号生产力大楼B座6层
邮　　编：100088
发行电话：010-82005927，010-82007837
网　　址：http://www.cicc.org.cn, http://www.thatsbooks.com
印　　刷：北京利丰雅高长城印刷有限公司
版　　次：2017年1月第1版第1次印刷
开　　本：155×230毫米 1/16
印　　张：14.5
字　　数：220千
定　　价：129.00元